What an
Art Director
Does

What an
Art Director
Does

An Introduction to
MOTION PICTURE
PRODUCTION DESIGN

Ward Preston

SILMAN-JAMES PRESS
Los Angeles

First Edition
10 9 8 7 6 5

Library of Congress Cataloging-in-Publication Data

Preston, Ward.
What an art director does: an introduction to motion picture
production design / by Ward Preston
p.   cm.
Includes bibliographical references and index.
1. Motion picture—Art direction—Vocational guidance. 2. Motion
pictures—Setting and scenery.   I. Title.
PN1995.9.A74P74   1994   791.43'0233—dc20   94-30605

ISBN: 1-879505-18-5

Cover design by Heidi Frieder

Cover illustrations by Peg McClellan

Printed and bound in the United States of America

SILMAN-JAMES PRESS
1181 Angelo Drive
Beverly Hills, CA 90210

In Memory of Frances Preston,
who didn't raise her boy to be a soldier

The MOTION PICTURE ART DIRECTOR
• HIS RESPONSIBILITIES, FUNCTIONS, AND ACCOMPLISHMENTS •

ART DIRECTOR IS ASSIGNED TO STORY BY THE PRODUCER.

SET CONFERENCE WITH THE PRODUCER AND THE DIRECTOR.

THOROUGH STUDY & RESEARCH FOR PURPOSE OF AUTHENTICITY.

ART DIRECTOR GIVES GRAPHIC FORM TO HIS CONCEPT OF SETTINGS.

COMPLETE ARCHITECTURAL DRAWINGS MADE BY SET DESIGNERS.

SKETCH ARTISTS SHOW, IN SKETCHES, HOW SETS WILL LOOK ON SCREEN

SCALE MODELS OF ALL SETS ARE BUILT BY MODEL ARTISTS.

PROPOSED SCHEMES FOR SETS APPROVED BY PRODUCER & DIRECTOR.

ESTIMATED SET COSTS ARE BUDGETED BY THE ART DIRECTOR.

ART DIRECTOR'S PLANS ARE APPROVED BY PRODUCTION MANAGER.

ART DIRECTOR AIDS IN "LOCATION" SELECTION OUTSIDE OF STUDIO.

PROGRESS OF SETTING CONSTRUCTION CHECKED IN WOODWORKING MILL.

SET CONSTRUCTION SUPERVISED BY ART DIRECTOR ON STAGES

MECHANICAL UNITS DEVELOPED FROM WORKING DRAWINGS.

ART DIRECTOR SELECTS PAINTS, WALL PAPERS, & SURFACE TEXTURES.

DIRECTION OF STYLE AND PLACEMENT OF SIGNS & LETTERING.

SCENIC ARTISTS PAINT BACK DROPS FROM DETAILED DRAWINGS.

PLASTIC ORNAMENT AND SCULPTURED UNITS REQUIRE DIRECTION.

SELECTION OF TREES AND SHRUBBERY FOR LANDSCAPING.

ART DIRECTOR SELECTS PLUMBING FIXTURES & DIRECTS INSTALLATION.

CARRIAGES, BOATS AND "PROPS" BUILT FROM DETAILED DRAWINGS.

ART DIRECTOR SELECTS FABRICS AND SPECIAL DRAPERY MATERIALS.

LIGHTING FIXTURES OF PROPER PERIOD DESIGNED & SELECTED

INTERIOR DECORATIVE FURNISHINGS SELECTED AND APPROVED.

ART DIRECTOR DETERMINES PROPER PLACEMENT OF BACK DROPS.

CONFERENCE WITH DIRECTOR REGARDING MONTAGE SEQUENCES

PROCESS AND "TRICK" SHOTS REFLECT TECHNICAL TRAINING & EXPERIENCE

CAMERAMAN AND ART DIRECTOR CO-OPERATE IN ILLUMINATION.

THE SET IS READY, AND PHOTOGRAPHY OF THE PLAY BEGINS.

PICTORIAL PERFECTION OF THE SETTING AIDS IN TELLING EVERY STORY.

An early example of the effort to clarify the somewhat ambiguous title of "art director" was this 1940's era drawing, which is attributed to the Warner Bros. illustrator Harold Cox.

Contents

Introduction

Everything you see

Perhaps the best way to introduce a book that promises to reveal the mysteries of motion-picture art direction is to recall my own curiosity as I show up for work on my first day as a draftsman in the art department of Warner Bros. Studios. The drafting room physically appears to be very much like that of any architectural office, yet the "feeling" is quite different. First, I am assigned a place amid the sea of drafting boards, and instead of a stool, a bench! This is the first surprise. Does this mean that my boss is actually going to sit down beside me as we discuss a drawing? So much for architectural protocol.

After settling into this anachronistic wonderland where drawings of spaceships and castles share space with skyscrapers and Conestoga wagons, I am ushered into the office of Stanley Fleisher, the supervising art director. Although these are the declining days of the major studio system, his office reflects the glory that once was Caesar's, and he wears the vest and tie expected of one in his position. He bids me the expected warm welcome and proceeds to give me a thorough briefing on the work expected of a studio draftsman. I learn that my job title is now Set Designer and that I will

work for an art director very much as an architectural draftsman works for an architect. Feeling secure in going into a
job so well suited to my architectural training, I then dare to
pose the question that has been plaguing me ever since the
first time I noticed the credit on the screen. "Mr. Fleisher," I
ask tentatively, "what does an art director do?"

After what I presume to be reflective thought, he replies
proudly: "The art director is responsible for everything you
see on the screen . . ." he pauses to consider the modifying
clause: ". . . that doesn't move . . ." then, searching for a further amendment, wistfully adds: ". . . and is usually out of
focus."

Armed with this somewhat ambivalent philosophy of the
business I had ventured into, I then proceeded to spend the
next 25 or so years learning the trade. It is my hope that those
who are considering a career in art direction or even those
who are already in the motion-picture business will gain from
these pages a better appreciation of what an art director or
a production designer does.

If this otherwise academic endeavor tends to lapse peri-
odically into personal memoirs, I offer my apologies in
advance. They are the musings that make, for me, this unfamiliar chore of writing at least bearable. Indeed, if it weren't
for the opportunity this project afforded to recall some of the
wonderful war stories of our business, this book probably
would not have been written at all. Actually, there are two
people who bear the onus of this book's existence: first, my
son, Vernon Preston, for setting up this word processor to
tolerate my Lionel Hampton approach to typing, and sec-
ondly a thoughtful actor who unknowingly kept my career
alive when it might easily have taken another direction.

One of the first films I worked on was the classic detec-
tive-adventure story *Harper*. The producer of the show very
generously allowed the art director, Al Sweeney, to invite the
show's often forgotten set designers and their families to the

wrap party. For my wife, Beverly, this would prove to be a pleasant diversion, and it came just in time to appease her recent reminders: "You didn't spend all that time in school and taking that licensing exam to become a studio draftsman. You are still an architect and isn't it about time that you thought about reopening your office?"

The party was wonderful. It was held on a soundstage in a replica of the Beverly Hills Polo Lounge that was built for the show. With the mood lighting, catered food, and enthusiastic musicians, it was probably a better setting than the lounge itself. We, the show's four set designers and our wives, were convened at a perimeter table, taking in the "celebrity intensive" crowd with all the *savoir-faire* of a tour group from Des Moines. At the bar were most of the principals of the show, including Paul Newman, Lauren Bacall, Shelly Winters, Robert Wagner, Arthur Hill, and Julie Harris.

Emboldened by the generous portions of champagne being served by the wandering waiters, one of our group (to this day he pleads sobriety) ventured to the star-laden bar and volunteered the answer to the question that he was sure had been consuming them with curiosity. "Why yes, the people who designed this exceptional set are here tonight. In fact, we are all sitting at that table right over there." Whether it was to avoid a scene, or because he really has the sensitive personality he exhibited that night, Paul Newman accompanied our loquacious spokesman back to the table. He spent a full 15 or 20 minutes sitting with us, explaining to our wives what really talented people they had married and charming each of them with personal questions and quips. I never again was prodded to abandon my studio career in favor of "that stuffy old architectural business."

The History of Art Direction

With apologies to E.G.E. Bulwer-Lytton.

I t was a dark and stormy night as he crouched close to the dank wall of his all-too-familiar lair. In the background is the comforting crackle of the communal fire and the chant of the tribal elder as he retells the legend of the Great Hunt. Drog smiles to himself as the children react to the spear-wielding storyteller's animated gestures. His permanently stained fingers reach for another piece of charcoal, and he returns his attention to the gathering herd of bison on the cave wall.

The plight of his fellow slaves toiling around him gives Abu pangs of guilt as he carves the bas-relief images into the massive limestone block. Could it be that his Egyptian master is becoming more tolerable? Or is he really beginning to enjoy the daily tales of the Pharaoh's exploits? Signing his work never occurs to him.

Fra Dominico cherished his sequestered existence. It is not everyone who can express his love for the faith by illuminating the word of God. With each controlled stroke of the expertly carved quill and delicate placement of each treasured fragment of gold leaf, the manuscript takes on a glowing radiance to match the spirit of the narrative.

These melodramatic vignettes are admittedly off the wall, but for me, they best describe the roots of the career we have come to know as art direction: *the enhancement of communication by visual means.* I submit that this definition would hold up even for the efforts of caveman Drog. And that was at a time when a picture was only worth a hundred and fifty-seven words!

The origins of motion-picture art direction obviously can't predate the invention of the medium, but you can be sure that it wasn't too long after Thomas Alva Edison developed his first film strip that he started looking for someone to paint a scenic backing. Even the filming of the Corbett-Fitzsimmons fight of 1897 involved some art direction. A banner proclaiming the Veriscope copyright was designed and applied to the apron of the boxing ring. By the turn of the century, Edison had built a studio and enlisted the talents of noted artist Hugo Ballin to design his sets.

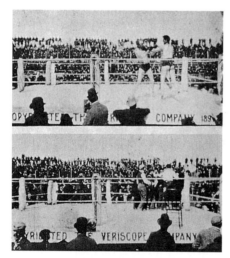

The earliest ventures into filmmaking required a degree of art direction. Here, the banner stating the Veriscope copyright is applied to the ring of the 1897 Corbett-Fitzsimmons bout.

It is only natural to expect that the first efforts at motion-picture art direction will emulate its parent medium, the theater. The proscenium arch might be missing, but backdrops, the profile cutouts, and the flared sidewalls all hearken to the discipline of stage design. Indeed, the cinematic dictum of maintaining the "line" (to keep the audience oriented with the action) owes its genesis to the psychology of proscenium-inhibited audiences.

Outdoor filming on spectacular locations doesn't obviate the need for art direction. *The Great Train Robbery* of 1903 painfully proves this point. The scenic splendor certainly enhances the story, but when the action moves into the poorly conceived cabin and telegraph office, the storytelling spell is broken. Making these real backgrounds blend

*The great outdoors is featured in the landmark film **The Great Train Robbery**. It's the natural vistas that set movies apart from their parent art form, the stage.*

The abrupt cut to the plight of the telegrapher in the same film, however, leaves little doubt that we are really looking at a staged presentation. The set is very theatrical. (Note the clock painted on the wall.)

seamlessly with the created settings has been a challenge to art directors ever since the first camera went outdoors.

Sometimes, the art director has the opportunity to create the awe-inspiring vistas himself. Known since the beginning of filmmaking as "spectacles" these are the pictures that bring the kudos and the glory, where the audiences leave the theater humming the sets! The first spectacles to appear on film were from Europe. In 1913, both *Les Miserables* and *Quo Vadis* arrived in this country and received popular acclaim. It wasn't too much later, in 1916, that D.W. Griffith met the European challenge with his landmark production of *Intolerance*.

*The D.W. Griffith spectacle **Intolerance** showcased the work of the art director. The Babylonian palace sequence required a balloon-mounted camera crew to capture its splendor.*

Griffith's introduction of close-ups, medium shots, and inserts to contrast with the master shot marks a giant step forward in cinematic technique. But, of greater interest to art directors are the mind-boggling sets he had built for *Intolerance.* The Babylonian palace of Belshazzar was an eclectic potpourri of architectural styles with grand stairways rising to dizzying heights. And even these monumental stylobates are dwarfed by the colonnades soaring above. Now there's a hummer!

The title Art Director took some time in emerging. The first sets were often designed by a master carpenter. When the demands of historical or regional accuracy exceeded the experience of the builder, the designing was done by an Artistic Executive or a Technical Director. Later, the title Art Director was borrowed from the publishing business and seemed to capture the spirit of the job. Even after the title came into common usage, it seldom appeared as a screen credit. In 1916, an article in *Photoplay* popularized the work of art directors, noting that this recently created profession had "come to stay" and that to qualify for the job, one should be "a well-read and much-traveled gentleman who has broken bread in the poor man's hovel and wine glasses in the rich man's palace." Fortunately, this criteria never found its way into the union bylaws.

Art directors, like many others in the film industry, eschew the caption "unionist." So, as the writers, actors, and directors formed "guilds," cinematographers, editors, and art directors formed "societies." Today's Society of Motion Picture and Television Art Directors is also Local 876 of the International Alliance of Theatrical and Stage Employees. The genesis of the Art Directors' Society goes back to 1924, when the community of Hollywood art directors started getting together on a regular basis, and, in the spirit of good fellowship, drew up a charter proclaiming themselves as the Cinemagundi Club. This tongue-twisting name was inspired by the artists' group in New York called the Gundi Club.

The advent of the Talkies in 1927 would not seem to have much of an effect on the visual aspect of filmmaking. However, it was a milestone event that brought with it the demand for more sophisticated storytelling and a commensurate improvement in the believability of the sets. It was also in this year that the Motion Picture Academy was established, giving added impetus to the art director's desire for excellence. Incidentally, it was the art director Cedric Gibbons who designed the Oscar statuette.

The continuing history of art direction is best outlined from 1927 on by reviewing the annals of the Academy of Motion Picture Arts and Sciences. The first award for art direction goes to William Cameron Menzies. It is given on the basis of his design for two films: *The Dove* and *Tempest.* With those interesting titles in mind, one might imagine that dichotomies counted for something in the first Academy Awards.

The decades of the '30s and the '40s encompassed what many think of as the Golden Age of the Movie Studios. Consider some of the art directors of this period: Richard Day (*How Green Was My Valley*), Lyle Wheeler (*Gone With The Wind*), Perry Ferguson (*Citizen Kane*), Cedric Gibbons (*Pride and Prejudice*), Alexander Golitzen (*Phantom of the Opera*), Hans Dreier (*For Whom The Bell Tolls*). Admittedly, some of these legendary designers were functioning as Supervising Art Directors at the time of their awards, but they also had noteworthy careers to confirm their creative abilities. (Supervising Art Director was a position created at each of the major studios to recognize the outstanding abilities of one of their staff and to give a continuity of style or a "look" to that studio's product. However, in later years, it sometimes became more of an administrative position and subject to the scorn of the principal art directors as they had to share their credit with someone not actively involved with the designing of the picture.)

William Cameron Menzies had already won the first Academy Award and been nominated for two others when **Gone With The Wind** *was released. Since "production designer" was not as yet an accepted credit, he was honored with a special award.*

Inspired by Orson Welles, art director Perry Ferguson created sets for **Citizen Kane** *on a minimum budget. The use of strategically placed elements and panels of black velvet allowed the viewer's imagination to fill in the voids.*

*A hillside in the San Fernando valley was the empty canvas that art director Richard Day had to work with when he created the Welsh coal mining town for **How Green Was My Valley**.*

By the end of the '30s, the fascination with movies made in color and the high production budgets associated with these projects gave them what seemed to be an unfair advantage over films made in black and white. Therefore, in 1940, the Academy saw fit to split the category of Art Direction, giving separate awards for films made in color and for films made in black and white. With the exception of two years (1957 and 1958), this practice lasted until 1966, when it became obvious that the full-color film was the rule rather than the exception. Today, the designer may use the absense of color as a stylistic technique and will, ironically, pay a premium to work in this "obsolete" medium.

The emergence of television in the '50s shook the major studio system to it very roots. The transformation of the motion-picture industry that followed has not really been resolved to this day. TV variety shows and live dramas created a demand for art directors versed in stage design. Motion-picture art directors steer clear of the new medium until the advent of filmed series and movies made for television called for their cinematic experience.

The rise of independent productions in the '60s along with the increasing demand for product to fill television time cast to the winds what was left of the major-studio system. Those art directors who had worked most of their careers for a single studio found themselves working free-lance, setting up new office space for each new project, and, for the first time, taking on agents. Although this process was inherently disruptive and costly, the benefits of the situation were the revitalization of a closed-door industry, the disappearance of rampant nepotism, and opportunities for talented young people to enter the "business of show."

As you will see in a future chapter, today's art directors come from varied backgrounds. Although most of those who become established as art directors and production designers are contented with this satisfying career, a notable few have reached for broader horizons. Years ago, an English art director decided to have a go at directing. It worked out so well, that he moved to the United States and made a name for himself as Alfred Hitchcock.

The Art Department

"Yes, Virginia, there used to be one."

As long as we're in an historical mood, let's take a walk through a typical major-studio art department. Facilities such as these are virtually nonexistent today, but the visit is guaranteed not to be a waste of time. The functions that were addressed by the personnel of this vanishing institution are still worthy of consideration today.

You would expect the reception area for a successful major-studio art department to be decorated in the Art Deco style reflecting the Golden Age of Hollywood films with beautiful secretaries surrounded by tastefully mounted illustrations, elaborate model sets, and Oscar-laden glass shelves. These are images easily brought to mind, and, certainly, this would be the depiction if a movie were ever to include "Interior, Studio Art Department." However, the reality was that the art department's entire reception staff was usually a "Girl Friday" who handled all the calls, letters, and reception chores amid conservative, if not Spartan, surroundings.

Adjoining the reception area was the office of the aforementioned **Supervising Art Director**. As an art director of proven ability, it was his responsibility to be familiar with every film currently in production and to protect the studio

*The art department drafting room at Warner Bros.
First National studios in the early '30s was a bit less
glamorous than the Art Deco settings that emerged
from here. Photo: Courtesy of Frank Grieco.*

from the extravagances of over-zealous art directors as well
as from the mediocrity and "phone-it-in" carelessness often
bred by large institutions. He would read every new script
under consideration by the studio and give his opinion of the
visual opportunities it offered, the production challenges it
presented, and who on their staff of art directors might best
be assigned to the project. This position is now nearly nonexistent and although it may have rankled many of the staff
art directors who had to share a screen credit with this department head, they would be the first to admit that his
prestige in the front office often gave them the needed leverage to settle budget disputes with the unit production
managers.

Individual **Art Director's** offices were, of necessity, quite
large. A conventional desk was needed only as a resting place

for the telephone and as the receptacle for a camera, extra film, and a bottle of aspirin. The important elements of the office were the drawing board, the art-supplies cabinet, research files, and the wall-to-wall tack boards. There was never enough shelving for research books or layout spaces for drawings, models, or sample materials. Depending upon the scope of the show or the needs of the art director, this office was sometimes shared with an assistant art director, a continuity artist, or a set illustrator.

On a typical show, the art director would be assigned according to his specialty—such as musicals, military, science-fiction, historical period, high-style romance, light fantasy, or the ever-popular westerns. After reading the script and assimilating the research, he would generally make a tour of potential sets standing on the backlot or on soundstages. (In the glory days of the studios, some of the low-budget films would be shot entirely on existing sets!)

Once the survey of standing facilities was made, it was time for the location scout. Then as now, the location excursion was the perk that made all the frustrations of this business worth enduring. It was said that an hour away from the studio was like a week in the country, especially during the frenetic era that was dominated by such moguls as Jack Warner, Harry Cohn, and Louis B. Mayer.

On those occasions when the art director was scouting for locations or otherwise kept away from the art department, it became the duty of the **Assistant Art Director** to maintain the momentum of the pre-production activity. As an assistant art director, one was expected to manage the team of set designers, ferret out stock units, supervise set construction, and generally assume the duties of art direction, allowing the art director more time for meetings, location surveys, and time by the camera. (As will be noted later, when the title Production Designer becomes adopted by more and more art directors, the activities of the assistant art

As in an architect's office, the drafting room at Universal Studios is staffed by people who can transform ideas into orderly construction drawings. The difference is that this idea just might be a Medieval castle!

director remain pretty much the same, but he or she will assume the title of art director.)

The principal habitat of the assistant art director was usually the **Drafting Room**, which consisted of from 10 to 40 drawing boards. There, he supervised the work of a team of **Set Designers** who were assigned to his picture. Set designers were the draftsmen who made the working drawings (blueprints) from which were constructed the sets, props, furniture, vehicles, or location structures that made up the setting for a show. Unfortunately, the job was not as free-wheeling as the title might imply. The conceptualizing and preliminary sketching of a set was always done by the art director. From this information, which could vary from a sketch on a napkin to a fully rendered illustration, it was the set designer's job to transfer that concept to a measurable, orderly drawing from which the backlot craftsmen could

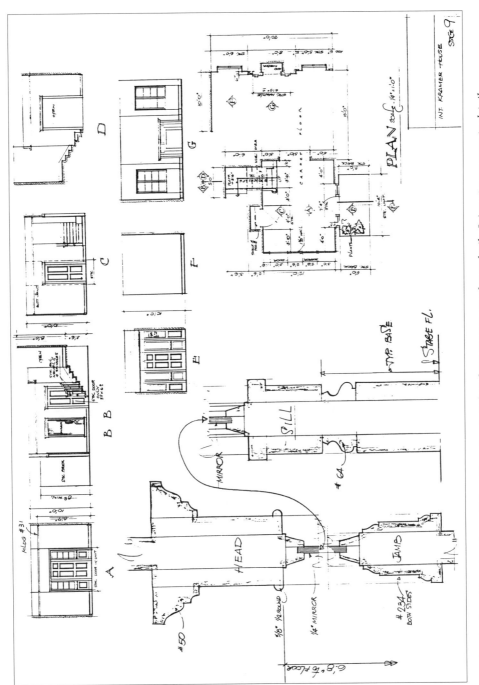

A typical working drawing will provide only enough information to get the set built. It is not necessary to detail stock units or to specify colors or wallpaper, which will be selected later. Drawing: Courtesy of Joe Hubbard.

work. This often included the finding and measuring of stock mantels and doorways, etc., which were squirreled away in the studio's storehouse or "scene dock."

The drafting room itself was truly a wondrous space. Models, illustrations, and props reflecting the various films in production were everywhere. Wall displays included samples of moldings, brackets, and other architectural details. These samples were an important part of the design process, and a generous space was set aside for their display and storage. A full-sized "ruler" along each wall was a great aid in visualizing spaces at full scale.

Too many people, even those who should know better, assume that the plans for motion-picture sets and locations were generated by an anonymous force somewhere in the shadows of the backlot. Even though they were often omitted from the screen credits, the talented people who prepared these working drawings were every bit as involved in the production of a picture as the assistant director who guides extras through a crowd scene. It was from these latter-day ateliers that emerged the towering spirals for Busbey Berkely's satin-clad dancers, the anguish-filled decks of the *HMS Bounty*, and the seductive Art Deco boudoirs of Jean Harlow and Joan Crawford.

The person in charge of the drafting room had a separate office and usually carried the title **Chief Draftsman** or sometimes **Drafting Room Art Director**. Very often, it was the endorsement of the chief draftsman that was needed for a set designer to get "off the boards" and up the ranks to the cherished position of Assistant Art Director. This was the icebreaker that it took to join the Society of Motion Picture and Television Art Directors.

The art-department aces were the set **Illustrators.** An art director could come across as a genius or fall flat on his face based on the art work he carried into a presentation meeting. Illustrators seldom had a common room. You would find them sequestered in fascinating offices and nooks as varied as their personalities. They reinforced their right to such idiosyncrasies every time they emerged with a freshly completed, breath-taking illustration.

Motion-picture set illustrators usually have backgrounds in fine arts or advertising art and must have the ability to make accurate perspective drawings that depict a set or location exactly as the camera will see it. The concession to the mathematical laws of perspective does not always sit well with the aesthetic psyche, but once he masters this exacting science, the artist can become almost evangelical in his devotion to its beautiful discipline.

I recall the incident of the illustrator who was having his work-in-progress reviewed (this imposition alone is enough to pique most artists) by a martinet of an art director. The artist was bearing up fairly well under the critique until his less-than-diplomatic boss suggested that the vanishing points were incorrectly placed. With a flourish that would have done D'Artagnan proud, the outraged artist withdrew an extra-sharp pencil from his tray and proceeded, with straight-edge accuracy, to etch into this nearly finished masterpiece the extension of each vanishing line to its properly positioned vanishing point. The stunned art director watched incredulously as the work was irreparably scarred and was left speechless when the vindicated artist packed up and departed. By the way, that exasperated artist was Gary Meyer, who is today on the faculty of the prestigious Art Center College of Design teaching illustration and, of course, perspective drawing.

Scale models were once an expected part of an art director's presentation. Their benefits seem obvious, but they are seldom used today. The art-department model shop was, if nothing else, an aromatic change of pace. The lair of the **Model Maker** emitted the blended fragrances of freshly cut wood, rubber cement, and lacquer-based paints that may be

*The art-department
models are not to be
confused with the
photominiatures made
in the prop shop. Harold
Fuhrman's presentation
models might be
described as 3-D
illustrations.*

*The camaraderie engendered by a large art department cannot
be denied. These renegades from local architects' offices were
likely candidates for the inevitable drafting-room gags.*

classified as pollutants today, but they were as welcome, in their own way, as the emanations from a corner bakery, a service station, or a shoe-repair shop. When the studio model shops were phased out, it was the set designers who were called upon to do their work.

An acknowledged master of the model making art was Harold "Snuffy" Fuhrman. Not only did he build exquisitely detailed set models, but he was also famous for his inventive practical jokes. With all those tools at hand, his idle moments became the concern of every potential gag subject in the art department. Stories are still told about the new set designers who were initiated to Snuffy's world of retractable coat hooks, balsa-wood cannonballs, and strategically placed air jets in the drafting room.

Blueprints aren't blue. They once were. When light is projected through tracing paper onto a paper coated with photosensitive emulsion, the image is transferred and can be revealed by a wet developing process not unlike that used in photography. The resulting "print" is blue over most of the surface and white only in those areas protected from exposure, as beneath a pencil line. The blueprinting process was phased out after World War II, when the Ozalid system of dry developing gained favor. These new ammonia-cured "blueprints," however, were actually white with lines of black, blue, or sepia. Now there are Xerox copiers capable of reproducing large drawings faster, clearer, and more fade-resistant than before. They can even enlarge or reduce the prints if necessary. At any rate, most studios had a blueprint room and a full-time **Blueprinter**, who often doubled as the art department **File Clerk.**

Files were no small part of a busy art department. Working-drawing files alone required considerable space. Cabinets containing 8x10 set stills were common to most art departments. The Scene Dock and the drafting room had matching files that catalogued the many reusable stock units. Of course, it was usually the memory of the scene dock manager that took precedence over the files. "Oh yeah, that saloon backbar was moved over to Stage 16 last week for a wrap party." Location photos, at least those taken by art directors, were kept in the art department also. Location departments had their own photo files, and they also were available to art directors.

One of the largest accumulations of files in any studio was in the **Research Department**. Although this facility was available to writers, directors, and many others, the art directors were its best customers. Some of the research collections amassed by the studios still exist. The Burbank Public Library adopted the Warner Bros. research files when they were in danger of being abandoned, and I believe that UCLA took the files of set stills under their wing.

When a studio was in full operation, a gallery of **Stage-Condition Plans** was imperative. These plans,which showed the size and exact position of each set on every stage, together with backlot layouts and scheduling charts, were used in daily meetings to organize the studio's filming and set construction. At Universal Studios, the center of this activity was appropriately called "The War Room."

Although these facilities are described in the past tense, the remnants of some art departments still exist at the rental studios in the Southern California area. The preponderance of independent production today, however, dictates that each project start from scratch, with the "art department" being a couple of offices rented for the duration of the show.

Art Directors' Training

"Are you sure Alfred Hitchcock started like this?"

Considering the many disciplines involved in creating the settings for a film, it's not surprising that art directors should come from varied backgrounds. More significant than their differences, however, are their commonalities. An artist's background and training are the most obvious requirements. Therefore, an ability to share ideas by way of sketches is an expected attribute of motion-picture art directors. An understanding of color, line, form, composition, and perspective is essential. This training plus a knowledge of history and a sense of the appropriate are the touchstones of the profession. Recognizing that the ability to communicate visually is the basic requirement for anyone who aspires to be an art director, let's explore some of the backgrounds we find in the profession today.

Stage designers for the theater would appear to have a head start in the preparation for motion-picture design. However, surprisingly few of the current motion-picture art directors (as opposed to television art directors) come from the ranks of this kindred medium. The theater's emphasis on illusion and fantasy seems to be in conflict with filmmakers'

*Awards shows and television specials are the province of those
art directors with a theatrical flair. Movie musicals also
demand the talents of these specialists. Photo: Courtesy of
Robert Keene Assoc.*

insistence on believability and reality. This has not always
been the case. As noted earlier, some of the earliest designers for motion pictures were alumni of the New York theater.
It was the advent of talkies and the concurrent emphasis on
realism that changed the focus of all aspects of this new
medium of motion pictures.

Fortunately, the introduction in the '30s of the musical
spectaculars kept the field open to these talented creators of
magical illusion. Today, television offers to those designers
with theatrical training the popular genres of variety shows,
game shows, and awards specials. Stage designers also have
thrived in the milieu of the three-camera audience shows as
well as the serialized daytime dramas.

One of those to successfully make the transition from stage
to film design is production designer Charles Rosen. He tells
of one of his earliest film credits bringing into play his the-

ater background. For the outrageous "Springtime for Hitler" musical-theater sequence in the Mel Brooks comedy *The Producers*, Chuck used a small Broadway playhouse normally devoted to dramatic presentations. To give the illusion of a recessed orchestra, he removed the first three rows of seats and built a railing around the nonexistent pit. The music, of course, was on a playback system, and with the help of the glow from some unseen music-stand lamps, the effect of a full theater orchestra was complete. The only complaint came from the actor who played the conductor. He had the uncomfortable job of leading this ghost band while kneeling as if he were standing in the pit.

Illustrators and continuity artists have the advantage of being masters of the most glamorous part of art direction: the "presentation." There was a time when union rules forbade art directors from making their own presentation drawings in an effort to promote more work for those brother members who worked exclusively as continuity artists or set illustrators. It seems ludicrous to have someone upgrade himself from illustrator to art director and then take away the very tool that got him there, so this rule is generally overlooked. Some of the best art directors and production designers in the industry today are former illustrators and "sketch artists" (the somewhat limiting title once pinned on motion-picture illustrators).

Production designer Robert Boyle, the recognized torchbearer for the profession of art direction today, began his film career in 1932 as a "sketch artist" at Paramount. Boyle's credits include the Hitchcock masterpieces *North By Northwest* and *The Birds*. With his solid grounding in the areas of illustration, continuity sketching, and matte painting, Bob would not hesitate to suggest shots that these disciplines made possible. One of his finest accomplishments was a composite matte shot made for *The Birds*.

Starting with a full-color illustration showing the desired
results (a bird's-eye view of the town under siege as a car
explodes in a gas station), Bob then storyboarded the various pieces needed to make that composite. That entailed
everything from a backlot gas station to a down-shot of diving birds to a matte painting of the entire fictional town. To
complicate an already difficult shot, Bob also had to coordi-
nate the fire and smoke effects especially as they crossed the
matte lines along with the soaring birds. The shot is all the
more remarkable when considering the absence of the digital technology available today.

Assistant art directors form the pool from which many
art directors are drawn. It is in this job that the apprentice-
ship for art direction is most valuably spent. Whether coming
from illustration, set decoration, architecture, or set design,
one won't get the practical experience of doing budgets,
breakdowns, or construction supervision until he or she becomes active as an assistant art director. The added
responsibilities of making on-the-spot construction decisions
for an absent art director and participating in location surveys and presentation meetings all help to prepare the future
art director or production designer for that first solo outing.
As an art director or production designer becomes more
comfortable with his assistant, it is not uncommon for him
to entrust in a talented aide some of the design functions
inherent in a big production. Such chores as laying out signs,
designing stairway details, or designing minor props and sets
will often become the duties of a trusted assistant. As mentioned earlier, it is also the assistant's job to keep the set
designers informed and busy.

Set designers (they carry the title most laymen would
associate with the work of an art director) are the draftsmen
who create the working drawings (blueprints) for motion-

*Production Designer Robert Boyle (he still respects the title of Art Director) supervised one of the most complicated composite shots of its time for Alfred Hitchcock's **The Birds**. Painting by Al Whitlock. Courtesy of The Margaret Herrick Library of the Academy of Motion Picture Arts and Sciences*

picture sets. Their background is usually in architectural drafting and those with aspirations of becoming art directors will
cultivate whatever sketching or rendering talents they may
possess. Here, again, the ability of an art director to make
occasional working drawings, although frowned upon by the
union, is an asset that cannot be ignored. Architects who
come into the film business generally find their way to the
job of art director through their experience as set designers
and assistant art directors.

Set decorators sometimes elect to assume the expanded
responsibilities of an art director. They are already familiar
with the research and preparation necessary to bring a visual "look" to a film. They almost universally have a
well-honed sense of taste and are very familiar with the psy-
chological influence that visual elements bring to a show. All
of this experience notwithstanding, the move into art direction is not as easy a transition as it may seem. Often, the
demands of construction supervision alone are enough to
discourage the most talented of these artists. Those who have
successfully made the change bring with them a rich background in the practice of fine tuning a completed set.

Film schools are just beginning to recognize the role of
the art director as part of the fabric of the motion-picture
industry. When this move to include a design curriculum in
the training of filmmakers is complete, it will surely enhance
both the quality of films as well as the effectiveness of the
art director. When a young artist sees film design as a direction for his or her talents, a program in art direction at a
recognized film school will be a welcome avenue to explore.
Such a program will put these students in contact with the
people who share their interest in the broader goal of filmmaking. Also, the inclusion of design courses in a film school
will give those film students concentrating on cinematogra-

phy, writing, editing, or directing the opportunity to better understand the discipline of art direction.

Since no such degree as Bachelor of Film Design exists, I'll take the liberty of proposing a hypothetical curriculum:

First Year

> Evolution of the Motion Picture
> Music Appreciation, Philosophy
> History of Art, History of Architecture
> Architectural Drafting, Freehand Drawing
> Designing for Motion Pictures I

Second Year

> Introduction to Motion Picture Production
> History of Motion Picture Design
> Interior Decoration, Creative Writing
> Computer Drafting, Perspective Drawing
> Designing for Motion Pictures II

Third Year

> The Business of Motion Pictures
> Set Construction, Location Facilities
> Special Effects, Computerized Photo Effects
> Illustrating and Storyboarding
> Designing for Motion Pictures III

Fourth Year

> Budgeting and Breakdowns
> Computer Design & Electronic Media
> Designing for Motion Pictures IV

The continuing course of Designing for Motion Pictures would cover the basics of research, layout, and camera angles in the first year and progress to the actual design and construction of sets along with the creation of visual effects in conjunction with other film students. Participating in the production of student films would bring an early awareness to the student of the art director's potential for contribution to the filmmaking process.

The ancillary courses such as special effects and computer design would not be expected to develop proficiency in these areas, but rather to expose the student to these specialty fields. To whatever extent the following chapters may contribute to the education of an art director or a production designer, this book still can not begin to satisfy the diverse requirements implied in the above curriculum.

Research & Clearances

"And don't call me Shirley."

Not too many years ago, in his acceptance speech for the Academy Award for art direction, the grateful recipient acknowledged the help of the research department. It is the one and only time that I can recall this group being publicly recognized for its contribution to filmmaking. For at least a year following that ceremony, you couldn't visit a research source without the incident being recalled. Research librarians finally had their much-deserved place in the sun.

The sources for motion-picture research can be as diverse as the subject matter itself. Fortunately, there are private libraries that specialize in gathering material of value to filmmakers. They will also contract with producers to read scripts and sort out references that might pose legal conflicts. Of particular interest to art directors are the research libraries' clipping files. Made up of photos from newspapers and periodicals, these files often go back many decades in their coverage. Whenever possible, make copies rather than borrow the original clippings. They often become shared research and beyond your dominion. Remember, these fragile artifacts are the lifeblood of the library and often are irreplaceable.

Research material comes in many forms. Trying to categorize and organize this Pandora's box of information is next to impossible as this typical interior of a designer's office will attest. Photo: Courtesy of Hub Bradon.

A comprehensive list of sources is impossible, but here are a few that immediately come to mind: the Warner Bros. Collection of the Burbank Public Library, Killam DeForrest Research Company (formerly the libraries of Paramount and MGM), Lillian Michelson Research Company, local public libraries, local historical societies, museums, the U.S. Government Printing Office, newspaper microfilm files, the Motion Picture Academy Library, specialty bookstores, newspaper and periodical stands, video-rental stores, Time/Life Books chronologies, pictorial history books, fashion magazines, architectural magazines (both U.S. and foreign), fine-arts books (coffee-table books), and, of course, the Historical Sears Catalog.

The subject matter for your search will always include architecture, interior decoration, and sign types. The script will suggest many other areas of research: i.e., historical period, military gear, western lore, or foreign locales. Even though it's not your immediate responsibility, additional research into wardrobe, vehicles, and hand props is important and is usually welcomed by others. Research material is especially helpful in concept meetings with the producer and director. And in production meetings, don't hesitate to pass out copies of your research along with plans and sketches.

Technical advisors are your best single source of research. Unlike a research book, they can respond to follow-up questions, and they are usually available to critique the work as it progresses. Often, they have access to research material unavailable to others. The value of an advisor during filming is generally acknowledged by the producer, but he will often have to be reminded of their need during pre-production. Not all shows hire technical advisors. Finding someone on your own can take you anywhere from the historical society to a local hardware store. The show's writer very often will have a list of contacts he has made during the course of researching the script. Suppliers of various props will gladly supply you with tech support, and if a project ever takes you to Small Town USA, you'll find more experts than you really need.

Hopefully, when doing a military show, you would be working with a retired serviceman who either had direct knowledge of the story you were telling or was keenly aware of all the military aspects of the show. With his help, you could expect to resolve not only the proper flags, insignias and vehicle markings, but also to get an insight into the ethnic and regional make up of the troops involved. These could prove to be valuable notations in the dressing of barracks and bunkers. Occasionally, technical advisors will nit-pick at trivial items, and they often become frustrated with the compromises that inevitably go with filmmaking. Art directors know that feeling.

Not everything you want to include in your research is mentioned in the script. To give a real vitality to the sets and locations, include design elements that will help establish a

ATSF DEPOT - OLPE, KANSAS

EMPORIA, KANSAS 1877

EMPORIA, KS APRIL 26-1895

SODEN'S CAMPGROUND

EMPORIA, KANSAS 1878

EMPORIA, KANSAS 1877

LYON COUNTY COURTHOUSE-1890

Turning the clock back to see Emporia, Kansas, as it was in 1921 at the time of **Mary White** *would be impossible without detailed research (see page 45). Photos: Courtesy of Walter M. Andersen.*

sense of time or place. Look up current presidents, contemporary personalities, world events, sports figures, product advertising, or anything else that can be visually associated with the story. Study the personalities of the scripted characters and wrap a life around them. Give them an alma mater, hobbies, interests, collections. A good director will gladly give you the time needed to "flesh out" a role. Art-department coordinators can usually be relied upon to help gather this information, but don't shortchange yourself on time to really dig in and study this material. It is the single-most important phase of the design process.

Photography may have been just a pleasant pastime before, but now as an art director, you will find it a valuable research tool. During the course of pre-production, never be without your camera. Design ideas are always popping up. From the unusual way that a wall lamp was installed with exposed wiring to the weather-beaten paint on a board fence, these visual realities should be available in your design palette. And, of course when you must match on the stage a portion of a practical location, photo details (usually including a ruler for scale) are necessary supplements to your field sketches and measured drawings.

It used to be a common practice to take time to shoot still photographs of every set just before the camera rolled. These "set stills" became a part of the art-department files and were not only an excellent source for studying stock units, but they also proved to be valuable as second-hand research. If you want photos (other than Polaroids) of the set and its dressing, either take them yourself or assign someone to this often-forgotten chore.

Legal research—the clearing of character names, places, publications, etc.—is usually handled by the producer's staff. However, knowledge of these clearances is critical to the operation of the art department. Indeed, many of the needs for clearances are generated by the art director. Fictitious

UNIVERSAL STUDIOS   **SIGN SHOP**

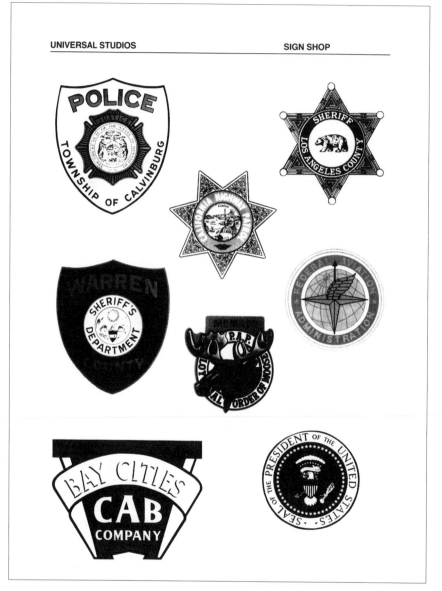

Although replicas of labels, tags, and decals can be bought from studio sign shops, the art department is often called upon to design fictitious emblems and logos. Catalog page: Courtesy of Universal Studios.

business signs, billboards, copyrighted posters, photos of per-sonalities, etc., typically fall into this category. It is advisable to find an art-department coordinator who can organize this necessary function.

In an effort to short-cut the red tape necessary for clear-ances on names such as those used on bulletin boards, it is often the practice to select names of crew members or rela-tives who would not object to having their names used on employees rosters or "wanted" posters. Try to avoid using the names of those crew members whose names will also ap-pear in the credits. With the extended credit lists we see today, that's not as easy as it once was.

The subject of product tie-ins is worthy of notice here as it bears directly on the matter to clearances. Most companies will gladly give permission for the use of their product on screen. Indeed, there is a specialized business focused on just this aspect of advertising. However, when a product or busi-ness is portrayed in an unfavorable light, either a clearance must be obtained or, more commonly, a fictitious product must be designed. The situation on films made for television is quite different. To avoid the perception of airing "free" ads on sponsored television, commercial networks like to see that all featured products and signs be fictitious. The argument over how this squares with the fact that most feature films (which are not subject to this taboo on brand names) even-tually show up on television anyway has never been resolved.

An interesting sideline to the above note on clearances occurred during pre-production for the comedy feature *Air-plane!* Whereas TWA was more than generous in its cooperation in the use of mock-ups, planes, and airport fa-cilities, they understandably did not want their name associated in any way with the zany operation portrayed in the story. A fictitious airline called Trans American was pro-posed, and the name was sent to research for clearance. They responded that in fact a cargo carrier by that name did exist. When contacted and informed of the nature of the film, they not only gave the necessary clearance, but insisted that their logo and corporate colors be used.

The idea of a glue-sniffing employee diving from a control tower window isn't exactly the image that an airline wants to project. Either invent a new company or get clearances. Photo: Courtesy of Paramount Pictures.

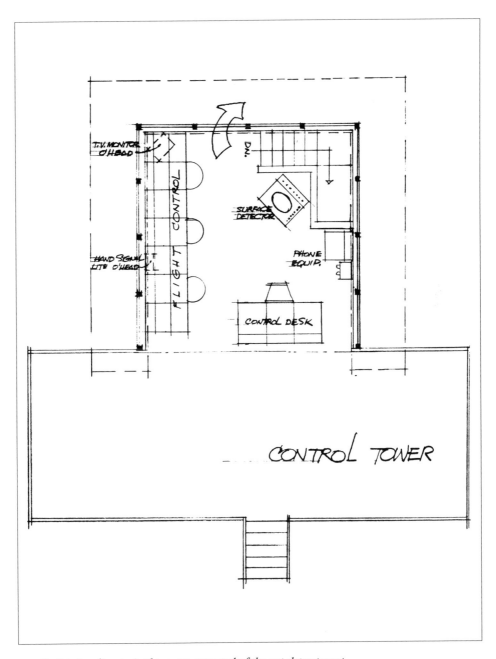

Script-size director's plans are expected of the art department.
The **Airplane!** sequence on the facing page was described in
this drawing, which shows the work platform as well as the set.

Breakdowns

Script, Nervous & Central Avenue.

O n the office wall of production manager Hal Herman hung a framed motto: *The cost will be remembered long after the quality is forgotten.* This attitude so irked an itinerant director that he had a wall hanging made for his own office: *The quality will be remembered long after the cost is forgotten.* The effort was not wasted. Hal appropriated the art work when the director left and hung it in his office as well. The art director is expected to satisfy both of these philosophies, and the script breakdown is the first step down this precarious path.

Considering all the times you are going to read, dissect, and reexamine the script, the first reading is probably the most important. Try to schedule enough time to read it in one sitting and hide any pencils, pens, or highlighters that are within reach. Savor the writing for the story itself and try not to anticipate the challenges that its production might present. A good screenplay in the hands of an articulate writer can motivate everyone associated with the project. The first reading of the script is not only a pleasant literary experience, it can also set the mood that will be sustained through the entire project.

INT/EXT

85 EXT. BILLY'S HOUSE - NIGHT   *STARTS INSIDE*

Jake retreats through the already demolished front door.
He pulls the pin on another grenade, smiling like a kid
on the Fourth of July. As the explosion rips through the
kitchen roof, Jake hurls the grenade through the front
door. Now, the front of the house explodes and bursts
into flames. Jake shouts triumphantly and stabs a
clenched fist into the night sky.

86 INT./EXT. SHERIFF'S CAR *EXT SHERIFF'S STATION*

Deputy Ray is breaking to a stop in front of a completely
dark sheriff's station. There's no missing the sound of
that distant explosion. Deputy Ray spins the steering
wheel and hits the gas. A distant plume of fire comes
into view.

87 INT./EXT. STATION WAGON *EXT. HWY REST STOP (SEE SC. 80)*

Sophia jerks her lips away from the canteen she's
drinking from. She sits up sharply in her seat. Her eyes
lock on the column of fire in the distance. As the
explosions echo around her, her shocked face starts to
fill with worst-case scenarios.

88 INT. BASEMENT

Flames roar into the basement in huge balls of fire which
drive Maggie and Reg back into the store room.

89 INT. STORE ROOM *(PART OF BASEMENT)*   *(SAME SET)*

Reg hits the light switch. Nothing happens. There's no
circuitry left upstairs. Maggie and Reg look frantically
around the store room. The room is lit only by pulsing
crimson flashes from the fire eating it's way through the
basement. The firelight shows one thing clearly: No more
doors. Just shelves lined with empty canning jars.

Maggie and Reg glance at each other. Their faces say We
Are Dead. Another explosion from above rocks them into
each others arms.

(CONTINUED)

*This hypothetical action sequence needed a little clarification to
put the events into the proper sets and locations. The fire and
stunts make this sequence a good candidate for a storyboard.*

Once the script has been read through and pondered for its potential visual impact, the time has come to reread the script for the purpose of making the budget breakdown. Using any method with which you are comfortable, highlight, underline, circle, or marginally note every scripted item or implied reference to the visual make-up of the picture. A good writer will introduce each new location with a helpful line or two of description. Stage direction that identifies doors, windows, closets, etc., will often dictate a room's layout just as a POV (a scene describing what an actor sees from his or her point-of-view) usually establishes a link between rooms or buildings.

Don't ignore the dialog when reading for a breakdown. The lines a writer gives the actors can sometimes reveal more about a set than his stage direction. To quote Bette Davis's immortal line, "What a dump!" Also, don't hesitate to question a line of dialog that might not be appropriate to the physical environment as you envision it. The director might have an interpretation of that line that will require you to re-think the design of the set in question.

It has become customary for assistant directors to draw a horizontal line on the page between each scene change. (In the art director's case, the break line can be at each change of set or location.) These lines not only give us a graphic organization of each page, but they also prove to be helpful in estimating the percentage of each page dedicated to any particular set or location. It is also customary to make this estimate in terms of eighths of a page. Personally, I never did get used to referring to a page-and-a-half of script as "one-and-four-eighths" pages.

Make your own script breakdown. Many others on the show will be making script breakdowns. While it may seem expedient to work from a handy numbered form, your own breakdown might reveal some location or set considerations that hadn't occurred to others: There may be scenes written

"BACKDOORS"
SAN FRANCISCO LOCATIONS

SCENES	NO	SET TITLE	D/N	LOC	PGS
1-10	300	INT-EXT CABLE CAR	D	HYDE ST.	3
20-27	—	EXT. TURNTABLE & BARN	N		2
28-29	100	INT. POLICE BLDG. CORR.	N	S.F. HALL OF JUST.	1¼
30-31	—	INT. CORONER'S AREA	N		3/4
32	—	EXT. S.F. STREETS (BELLS SEQ.)	D		¼
58-60	200	INT. POLICE GARAGE	D	S.F. HALL OF JUST	1
67-69	100	EXT. RICO'S STALL	D	FISHERMANS WHARF	2
70-71	100	EXT. COOPER BLDG	D	S.F. ALCOA BLDG	½
166-174, 85 78,126,147-155 231	—	INT. POLICE SQUAD RM.	D&N	S.F. HALL OF JUST	10
80-84	200	INT.-EXT TRENCH'S HOTEL & LOBBY	D	CHESTNUT ST.	4
86-93	—	EXT. RAINIES APT. & FOYER	D	3RD ST?	1¾
122-125	—	EXT. BOAT SLIP	D	SAUSALITO	4
127-129	100	EXT. S.F. STREET (HAROLD BUSTED)	D		1
130-133	100	EXT. S.F. ALLEY (FRIEND BUSTED)	N		½
140-146	—	INT. PROPERTY ROOM	D	S.F. HALL OF JUST	3
156-165	—	EXT. OLD GUN EMPLACEMENT	D	SAUSALITIO	4
175	—	EXT. PHONE BOOTH	N		⅛
179-206	100	EXT. S.F. STREET & ROOFTOP	DUSK?		4
226-230	—	EXT. McBRIDE'S HOUSE	N		7
241-243	—	EXT. S.F. STREET (McBRIDE TAIL)	D		3/4
244-247	200	EXT. BASEMENT RESTAURANT	D		1
251-303	550	INT-EXT WHARF & WAREHOUSES	D	PIER 47	8½

(63)

The first breakdowns are going to be subject to a lot of revisions. Before going to a hard copy, stay flexible with draft copies that group sets and locations by type, locale, or time period.

"BACKDOORS"

STUDIO & LOCAL LOCATIONS

SCENES	NO	SET TITLE	D/N	LOC	PGS
33-57	01	INT-EXT VIKING HOTEL	D	VENICE	8¼
103-112 176-178	03	INT-EXT NURSERY & PLAYGROUND	D	PASADENA	10
113-121 221-225	05	INT. HOSPITAL CORRIDORS	D&N	loc.loc } PASADENA	6
207-219	07	INT. HOSPITAL EMER.& I.C.U.	N	loc.loc }	4½
220-	09	INT. HOSPITAL COFFEE SHOP	N	" " }	1
304-313	11	EXT. COOPER HOME	N		1¼

(31)

72-77	02	INT. COOPER'S OFFICE	D	STAGE 16	8
94-102	04	INT. RAINIE'S APT.	D	STAGE 12	7
232-240	06	INT. POLICE PISTOL RANGE	D	STAGE 12	3
79-	08	INT. JAIL CELL	D	STAGE 2	2½
61-66	10	INT. CORONER'S VIEWING RM	D	STAGE 12	2
83	12	INT. TRENCH'S ROOM	D		⅛
134-139	14	INT. HOTEL LOBBY	N	STAGE 2	4½
248-250	16	INT. BASEMENT RESTAURANT	D	STAGE 16	4
	04	INT. CORONERS AREA			

(31)

for continuous action that have to be filmed on two or even three different sets or locations. Conversely, there may be scenes that are written for two or more different locations that could be filmed on one set or location that has all the elements needed for those various scenes.

It is wise at this point to look for "phantom sets." For example, images that appear on a TV monitor are not always stock footage, and they might require some pre-production or second-unit filming on sets that are not noted in the script as INT. TELEVISION NEWSROOM or EXT. SCENE OF THE ACCIDENT. These additional scenes will often involve set construction. Pre-production photo sessions to get still photos of the actors to be used as props or for set dressing will also require additional art-department work. Images seen on computer screens might not involve any sets, but the art director is responsible for supervising the creation of the graphics and custom programming necessary to produce those images.

After you have satisfied yourself that you have a handle on the physical requirements of the show, confirm with the assistant director that you have the same set titles and that the scene numbers scheduled to take place in each set are in agreement. Your marked-up copy of the script is going to become your bible. By the time you have gone through a number of concept meetings and script revisions, it may not be the tidiest document in the world, but it will be your single best reminder of all the design decisions you have made for the picture. When the inevitable colored pages of script revisions come through, it is sometimes easier to write in minor changes of dialog or character names than to transfer all of your notes to the new pages.

Although the primary purpose of the breakdown is for budgetary reasons, it can be of value in other ways. Once a page count is made of scenes to take place in each set (you might try using the eighth-page system noted above), the priorities become clear as to which sets deserve greater attention. Which locations will best sell the look of the show? Which sets work better on a stage rather than on location? Which sets require special effects? How many sets work at night? (A lot can be left to the imagination in the distant darkness of night sequences.)

Don't let the page-count alone determine your priorities in the allotment of the set-construction budget. Keep in mind that a relatively brief sequence in a set or location that is seen only once might have more of a visual impact on the audience than the action occurring in one of the more widely used sets. For example, cityscape locations deserve special attention as they are expected to tell not only the story of our principal characters, but also of the lives and circumstances of those around them. The street scene may only be used as an "establishing shot" or for a brief sequence of actors entering a building, but what the audience gleans from that limited exposure can do much to set the tone of the following scene, or indeed, the whole story.

In the Robert Radnitz television movie *Mary White*, it was important to reveal that Emporia, Kansas, in 1921 was a prosperous Midwest farming center when the *Emporia Gazette* publisher, William Allen White, wrote the famous eulogy upon the death of his teenage daughter Mary. Although the screen time for this location was minimal, producer Terry Nelson agreed that a substantial budget allowance should be made to transform a nearby Kansas town into the Emporia of 1921. It covered the cost of two billboards, a movie-house façade, a civic statue, and a gazebo for the park. The work proved to be worthwhile.

The art director's breakdown sheet should contain the **set title**, whether it's to be an **interior** or an **exterior** setting, for **day** or **night** sequences, **scene numbers** of the action to take place in each set, a **page count** of all the scenes to take place in each set, and the **estimated cost** to build or otherwise create that set. For cost-accounting purposes, each set or location is given a **set number**. Additionally, the breakdown sheet might include notes regarding **special effects** (snow, rain, fire, etc.) that may effect the set. As they become known, **locations** and **stage numbers** are added to the breakdown. Budget figures are usually more accurate if **rental costs** for such items as **greens, backings,** and **stock units** are listed separately.

Personally, I've found that identifying the action by listing the scene numbers on the breakdown sheet isn't really enough to jog my memory. I prefer to briefly recap the action on 3x5 cards. Sometimes I'll borrow the assistant director's technique of using a color code to highlight night work or special-effects sequences. I can take these cards on location scouts or I can leaf through them when I'm designing the sets. The new age of electronic notebooks and memo pads will surely antiquate this system, but I still find them handy to pin up on a tack board for an overview of the show.

A handy supplement to the construction budget is a **back-up sheet**, which synopsizes the work anticipated for each set or location. Not only does it remind you of the work you plan to do, but it also helps the production manager appreciate the scope of work needed to prepare a location for filming. All that this document needs to contain is the **set number**, the **location**, the **set title** with space to outline the **anticipated work**, and the **estimated cost**.

When making any kind of estimate, the greatest single factor in the process is experience. Keeping actual cost records of previous shows will allow you to arrive at a cost-per-square-foot price that can be applied to future projects. Since many sets are built upon an existing stage floor, it sometimes is more accurate to estimate the cost based on a unit price-per-square-foot of *wall area*. Hard ceilings, when they are used, can be computed just as additional wall surfaces. If floor coverings such as sheet vinyl, hardwood strips,

LIVING HIGH
SET LIST and CONSTRUCTION ESTIMATE

date

Producer	Nita Hitt		Miles Moore	Director
Prod. Mgr.	Les Money		Ward Preston	Prod. Dsnr.

No	Int/Ext	Set Title	D/N	Pgs.	Location	Scenes	Cost
1	Int./Ext	Smythe Mansion	D	6 1/2	Monticito	1-4	2500
2	Ext.	Yacht Club Pool	D	1 7/8	Yacht Club	5, 9, 18 pt.,19, 23, 25-27	600
3	Ext.	Yacht Club Cafe	D	3/4	Yacht Club	6, 10, 17	0
4	Ext.	Marina Walkway & Parking	D	1 3/4	Yacht Club	7, 28 - 29, 46, 78	0
5	Ext	Marina at "Vanguard"	D/N	9	Yacht Club	8, 50, 66, 78pt., 83	6500
6	Int/Ext	Aboard "Vanguard"	D/N	15	Travels	20, 31-36, 37-38, 41, 47, 52	12000
7	Ext.	Roadway at Tennis Courts	D	1 1/2	Yacht Club	11-14	1500
8	Ext	Yacht Club Front Gate	D	7/8	Yacht Club	15	300
9	Ext	Employee Entrance	D	1/2	Yacht Club	16	1500
10	Int	Poolside Cabana	D	1 7/8	Yacht Club	18, 24	3000
11	Ext.	Al's Vantage Point	D	1/2	T.B.F.	21, 26pt, 30	0
12	Int.	Animal Shelter	D	3/4	Humane Soc.	39	1300
13	Ext	Alley near Shelter	D	1/2	T.B.F.	40, 42	0
14	Ext	Channel at Calley Estate	D	5/8	Intracoastal	43	200
15	Int/Ext	Calley Estate	D/N	11 1/4	Spec House	43-45, 53-65	12500
16	Ext	Carol's Vantage Point	D	3/8	T.B.F.	45pt.	0
17	Int/Ext	Horse Auction Site	D	9	Paddock	48, 49	2500
18	Int	Carol's Hotel Room	N	1/2	T.B.F.	51	0
19	Ext.	Intracoastal Inlet	D	1/4	T.B.F.	67	0
20	Ext	Bahamas Airport	D	4 3/4	Lugo Field	68, 93, 97, 99, 101, 103, 106, 108-115	4000
21	Ext.	Nassau Harbor	D/N	3 3/4	Harbor	69, 77, 84, 86, 90-92, 95-96, 98, 100	13500
22	Ext/Int	Bahamas Hotel	D/N	3 1/2	Paradise Isle	70, 71, 87, 92	1200
23	Ext	Nassau Fishing Pier	D	2 3/4	Paradise Isle	72-75	1500
24	Int./Ext	Beachfront Bar	D	1/2	Paradise Isle	76	500
25	Int	Nassau Casino	N	3	Paradise Isle	79	1800
26	Ext	Nassau Backstreet Wharf	N	1 3/4	Harbor	80, 81	3500
27	Int	Nassau Police Station	N	1 3/4	Harbor	82	500
28	Ext	U.S. Customs Building	D	1/2	Cable Beach	88	800
29	Int.	U.S. Customs Office	D	3/4	Cable Beach	89	300
30	Int/Ext	Private Jet	D	1		94, 104, 109, 111, 113, 114	700
31	Ext	Road to Airport	D	2	Cable Beach	102, 105, 107	600
32	Int/Ext	Racetrack	D	8 1/2	Upson Downs	116-117	0
33	Ext	Beach	D	1/4	T.B.F.	22	0
				98 1/8		Set Construction	$73,300
						Backings	0
						Greens	1800
						Total	**$75,100**

Not included in the above estimates are location fees, the costs to strike sets, to patch and repair locations,
to build lighting scaffolds, nor the costs to build ramps, pits, or barriers for stunt work.

*The final construction estimate is still just that: an <u>estimate</u>,
often with locations yet to be found. However, be prepared to
live with these numbers. They become firmer by the day.*

LIVING HIGH

Construction Budget Detail

date

LOCATION	SET #	TITLE & ANTICIPATED WORK	BUDGET
Monticito	1	INT/EXT SMYTHE MANSION	2500
		Replant yard and garden	
Yacht Club	2	EXT YACHT CLUB POOL	600
		Build 5 canvas umbrellas	
Yacht Club	3	EXT. OUTDOOR CAFE	0
		Shoot as is	
Yacht Club	4	EXT MARINA WALKWAY & PARKING	0
		Shoot as is	
Yacht Club	5	EXT MARINA AT "VANGUARD"	6500
		Build Gazebo and Garden	
		Create area for horse trailer	
Travels	6	INT/EXT ABOARD THE "VANGUARD"	12000
		Add carpet overlay on top deck	
		Add wood veneer and top deck seating	
		Repaper interior	
		Recurtain windows	
		Remove antennas	
		Change name signs	
		Remove aftdeck windscreen	
		Replace shore boat	
Yacht Club	7	EXT ROADWAY at TENNIS COURTS	1500
		Erect prop stop signal	
		Place greens & fence as required	
Yacht Club	8	EXT YACHT CLUB FRONT GATE	300
		Place sign at guard gate	
		Rig gate to slam	
Yacht Club	9	INT/EXT EMPLOYEE ENTRANCE	1500
		Build time clock stand & card rack	
		Make signs to cover existing signs	
Yacht Club	10	INT POOLSIDE CABANA	3000
		Build 6 cabanas	
T.B.F.	11	EXT AL'S VANTAGE POINT	0

Backup sheets with recaps of work to be done not only tell the production department what you're up to, but also serve as handy reminders when prep-time becomes hectic.

Humane Soc.	12	INT ANIMAL SHELTER	1300
		Signs	
		Additional cages	
T.B.F.	13	EXT ALLEY NEAR SHELTER	0
Intracoastal	14	EXT CHANNEL at CALLEY ESTATE	200
		Sign to establish water taxi	
Spec House	15	INT/EXT CALLEY ESTATE	12500
		Build arbor for floral dressing	
		Build bandstand	
		Build walk-in safe	
T.B.F.	16	EXT CAROL'S VANTAGE POINT	0
Paddock	17	INT/EXT HORSE AUCTION	2500
		Build auctioneer's podium	
		Erect shade canopies	
		Make signs and banners	
T.B.F.	18	INT CAROL'S HOTEL ROOM	0
T.B.F.	19	EXT INTRACOASTAL INLET ("Vanguard" departs)	0
Lugo Field	20	EXT BAHAMAS AIRPORT	4000
		Make signs to cover existing signs	
		Build breakaway fence	
Harbor	21	EXT NASSAU HARBOR	13500
		Remove tire bumpers @ sea wall	
		Build "Strawmarket" booths	
		Add "Port of Nassau" signs	
		Add car rental signs	
		Cover existing signs	
		Paint tour carriages	
		Make gangplank to dock	
Paradise Isle	22	INT/EXT HOTEL	1200
		Signs	
Paradise Isle	23	EXT NASSAU FISHING PIER	1500
		Add signs & flagpole	
Paradise Isle	24	INT/EXT BEACHFRONT BAR	500
		Cover cafe signs	
Paradise Isle	25	INT NASSAU CASINO	1800

		Build frames for drapes	
		Bases for gaming tables	
Harbor	26	EXT NASSAU BACKSTREET WHARF	3500
		Make signs to cover existing signs	
		Repair gates	
		Add bumpers	
T.B.F.	27	INT NASSAU POLICE STATION	500
		Make signs and plaques	
Cable Beach	28	EXT U.S. CUSTOMS BUILDING (Nassau)	800
		Make establishing sign	
Cable Beach	29	INT U.S. CUSTOMS OFFICE (Nassau)	300
		Make signs and plaques	
T. B. F.	30	INT/EXT PRIVATE JET	700
		Add (and remove) logo on jet	
Cable Beach	31	EXT ROAD TO AIRPORT	600
		Make highway signs	
Upson Downs	32	INT/EXT RACE TRACK	0
		Shoot as is	
T.B.F.	33	EXT BEACH	0

TOTAL CONSTRUCTION BUDGET   **$73,300**

***NOT INCLUDED IN THE ABOVE ESTIMATES ARE LOCATION FEES, THE COSTS TO STRIKE SETS,
    TO PATCH AND REPAIR LOCATIONS, TO BUILD LIGHTING FRAMES,
    NOR THE COSTS TO BUILD RAMPS, PITS, OR BARRIERS FOR STUNT WORK.

or wall-to-wall carpeting are considered, they should be included at the current market price.

These estimating systems, which are a carryover from the construction trades, however, are not always applicable to the process of motion-picture set construction. The very nature of the unusual criteria that must be met by a motion picture set almost precludes the scientific approach to cost estimates. How much aging will the set require? How many duplicates of that breakaway window will be needed for the fight sequence? (For the film *The Towering Inferno*, we had to anticipate the added cost of building most of the sets of fireproof material. Ironically, the sets were better protected than the ill-fated building in the story.)

There are times when a "visualize-the-project" system seems to work best. Conjure up the work to be done from the first day through to completion. Visualize the size of the work crews and the duration of the job. Calculate that cost and add an equal amount for the cost of materials. This will give you a base number to add to or subtract from based on the unique conditions for that particular set. Is the crew familiar with studio-type construction? Will the set be built on a stage (familiar conditions), on location (possible weather delays), or on a makeshift stage (the use of warehouses and rental space where floor-nailing is impractical or forbidden will often dictate the use of weighted stage braces to support the walls). Will exotic materials be used or off-the-shelf builders supplies?

These considerations, along with an intuitive reaction based on previous experience, will usually give you as good an estimate as an item-by-item listing of labor hours and material quantities. However, for the new art director, my advice would be to make that grocery list and familiarize yourself with the cost of labor and materials in your area. Make your first estimates with the help of a builder or construction foreman. With a few shows under your belt, you won't have to

6 Int./Ext. *Vanguard* (3 of 4)   4 1/4 pgs

Scene	D/N	Action
77	N	On the afterdeck, Phillip and Al read of a local drug bust. Phillip gives Al a pep talk as they prep for the Casino. Al gets a phone call confirming his surveillance photos.
85	D	On the afterdeck, in Nassau, Phillip and Al consider the possibility of claiming the impounded drug money.
86	D	Lying in a stateroom, Carol overhears Phillip and Al plan to grab the impounded drug money.
91-92	D	Phillip and Al, jubilant over their coup at the customs office, are greeted by Carol with drugged coffee. Phillip calls Calley at the hotel to set up the money deal. After his call, he and Al pass out. Carol starts moving the bales.

---

7 Ext. Roadway at Tennis Courts   1 1/2 pgs

Scene	D/N	Action
11-14	D	Gatito breaks for freedom through the tennis court fence and shrubs, is done in by a racing car driven by agent Al. Jeeves witnesses the carnage from behind the fence. He retrieves only the rhinestone collar. Carol is the driver of the other car. She reverses her car to scold Al, then continues on to the employees' entrance as we peek at the photos and maps in her car.

Al on his way to main gate, Carol is going to service gate.

---

6 Int./Ext. *Vanguard* (4 of 4)   3 1/4 pgs

Scene	D/N	Action
96	D	Phillip and Al revive to find the remaining bales and the letter from Carol.
98	D	Phillip and Al read Carol's letter. She's the daughter of an old Calley partner. They decide to go to the airport.
118	D	The wrap-up: Jeeves reveals that he had a bundle riding on Cincinnatti Sam.

Sc. 77-98 take place in Nassau harbor.

---

8 Ext. Yacht Club Front Gate   3/4 pgs

Scene	D/N	Action
15	D	Al tries to bluff his way into the club. The guard doesn't buy Al's phony story and wont admit him ,but takes Al's bribe anyway.

Check: Guard shack? Drive -through? Walk on?

---

19 Ext. Intercoastal Inlet   1/4 pgs

Scene	D/N	Action
67	D	The *Vanguard* departs for Nassau. Al runs for the rail.

---

20 Ext. Bahamas Airport (2 of 2)   2 3/4 pgs

Scene	D/N	Action
103	D	Establish the jet preparing to taxi.
106	N	The jet waits behind another plane for takeoff clearance.
108	D	Cleared for take off, the jet begins to roll
110	D	The jeep arrives at the airport, spots the plane, crashes a gate to get to the runway, and begin their head-on run at the plane.
111pt	D	As the pilot looks. Phillip waves from the jeep. They close on each other.
112	D	The game of chicken heightens. The jeeps lights flash.
115	D	The climax of the show-down. They stop nose to nose.

Check planes, signs, etc. to establish Nassau

---

20 Ext. Bahamas Airport (1 of 2)   2 pgs

Scene	D/N	Action
68	D	A private jet is guided into a parking position on the tarmac next to a limo. Antony and Duke unload money bags.
93	D	As the jet is being prepped, Duke climbs aboard.
97	D	Calley sees his investors off on the jet. Carol drives up in Al's jeep, demands to be "let in on the deal".
99	D	Calley escorts Carol onto the plane.
101	D	Calley waves to the departing jet, boards a waiting helicopter with Duke.

---

21 Ext Nassau Harbor   1 3/8 pgs

Scene	D/N	Action
69	D	Amid the strains of a steel band and with tourists and a jeep rental stand nearby, the *Vanguard* pulls into port. Dock urchins grab the mooring line. They yank Al off the bow into the water.
84	D	Establish *Vanguard* in the harbor at dawn.
90	D	Phillip and Al arrive in the jeep. Start unloading the bales of government drug money.
95	D	Establish *Vanguard* as our heroes recover from the mickey.
100	D	Phillip and Al get another rental car, start for the airport.

When these 3x5 cards are not pinned up on the office tack-board, they are probably being taken on a location scout or being reviewed as preliminary sketches are drawn.

repeat that frustrating task, and you will have a better appreciation of the estimating process.

The pitfalls of early estimates are, for the most part, obvious. However, there are a few subtle traps that, with a little logic, can be anticipated. These costs can't necessarily be avoided, but they can sometimes be predicted and set apart from the usually fragile set-construction budget. For example, carpentry work that's needed for prop-truck shelves—and to prepare spaces for makeup, wardrobe, and property storage—can usually be expected when going to a new location. Grip work such as tarping in a day-for-night location often requires the help of the set-construction crew.

As a young art director working on his first solo outing, production designer Bill Creber was told that he was running over budget on a remote western set for the film *Rio Conchos*. In checking with the auditor, he found that the cost of grading an access road to the site was charged against the set-construction budget. Back in town, he reported to the supervising art director with an outraged account of the cavalier way the production manager had "robbed" him of his much-needed construction money. The older man just said, "Relax, kid. Welcome to the game!"

The costs of striking sets and of touching up rental locations are obvious expenses, but are often underestimated. Some rental studios will tack on a percentage of the construction cost as a "strike charge," whether they plan to strike the set or not. Often, on location, a local firm or individual will contract to remove various pieces of set construction. In the case of physical improvements to a site, they are often left as is. The value of the work can sometimes be negotiated as part of the location rental agreement. As mentioned earlier, the good will generated by thoughtful use of the host property will pay off later down the filmmaking road.

Among the first significant expenses on any show are the pre-production costs of set construction. Accordingly, the art director's budget is the first to meet the scrutiny of the production office. Keep both the production office and the director updated on the progress of the set construction, especially during the early phases of pre-production. Once the art director proves that he is aware of the budget and in control of his expenses, life becomes a lot easier, and any future suggestions of set modifications are placed in the context of serious consideration rather than capricious folly.

Hopefully, by the time the budget is needed, there will be a construction coordinator on board who can assist you in this less-than-exact science. This is where the previous association of the art director and the construction coordinator pays off. If they are familiar with each other's work habits, they know pretty much what kind of demands and compromises can be expected from one another. This can be very helpful when you consider that early budgets are based on the skimpiest of information: Not all of the locations have been established. Working drawings have not yet been drawn. Designs, when they exist, are still in sketch form. And in many cases, local sources for material and labor have not as yet been established.

The story continues to circulate about the art director who was lucky enough to have met his set-construction budget on a rather complicated picture. He was having cocktails at the wrap party with the show's assembled group of producers. One of them noted the accomplishment and asked the proud designer what the secret was to his rare talent. He grandly replied that it really was no secret at all. It is a time-proven formula used by all art directors: "You calculate the time allowed to finish the work multiplied by the weekly construction payroll plus the cost of materials and add ten percent for each additional producer on the picture." This story usually gets more laughs in the art department than it does in the production office.

LIVING HIGH

Construction Cost Report

As of   xx / xx / xxxx

SET #	DESCRIPTION	ACTUAL	BUDGET	(OVER) / UNSPENT
1	INT/EXT SMYTHE MANSION	2,866.56	2,500.00	(366.56)
2	EXT YACHT CLUB POOL	654.50	600.00	(54.50)
3	EXT YACHT CLUB CAFE		0.00	0.00
4	EXT MARINA WALKWAY & PARKING		0.00	0.00
5	EXT MARINA AT "VANGUARD"	6,715.24	6,500.00	(215.24)
6	INT/EXT ABOARD "VANGUARD"	8,065.47	12,000.00	3,934.53
7	EXT ROADWAY at TENNIS COURTS	845.00	1,500.00	655.00
8	EXT YACHT CLUB FRONT GATE	456.00	300.00	(156.00)
9	EXT EMPLOYEE ENTRANCE	846.25	1,500.00	653.75
10	INT POOLSIDE CABANA	2,462.66	3,000.00	537.34
11	EXT AL'S VANTAGE POINT		0.00	0.00
12	INT ANIMAL SHELTER	148.40	1,300.00	1,151.60
12A	INT ANIMAL SHELTER (cover set)	5,467.95	0.00	(5,467.95)
13	EXT ALLEY NEAR SHELTER		0.00	0.00
14	EXT CHANNEL AT CALLEY ESTATE	125.48	200.00	74.52
15	INT/EXT CALLEY ESTATE	11,600.76	12,500.00	899.24
16	EXT CAROL'S VANTAGE POINT		0.00	0.00
17	INT/EXT HORSE AUCTION SITE	1,732.50	2,500.00	767.50
18	INT CAROL'S HOTEL ROOM		0.00	0.00
19	EXT INTRACOASTAL INLET		0.00	0.00
20	EXT BAHAMAS AIRPORT	2,913.17	4,000.00	1,086.83
21	EXT NASSAU HARBOR	13,023.11	13,500.00	476.89
22	INT/EXT BAHAMAS HOTEL	879.50	1,200.00	320.50
23	EXT NASSAU FISHING PIER		1,500.00	1,500.00
24	INT/EXT BEACHFRONT BAR	1,264.89	500.00	(764.89)
25	INT NASSAU CASINO	1,902.13	1,800.00	(102.13)
26	EXT NASSAU BACKSTREET WHARF	2,865.00	3,500.00	635.00
27	INT NASSAU POLICE STATION	344.50	500.00	155.50
28	EXT U.S. CUSTOMS BUILDING	1,271.99	800.00	(471.99)
29	INT U.S. CUSTOMS OFFICE	384.29	300.00	(84.29)
30	INT/EXT PRIVATE JET	526.50	700.00	173.50
31	EXT ROAD TO AIRPORT	524.04	600.00	75.96
32	INT RACETRACK		0.00	0.00
33	EXT BEACH		0.00	0.00
	TOTAL CONSTRUCTION COSTS	**$67,885.89**	**$73,300.00**	**$5,414.11**

The more regularly that cost reports are updated, the better your chances are of meeting the budget. It usually takes the efforts of a full-time art-department coordinator to accomplish this.

Location Scouting

"Where shall we eat lunch?"

Y ou really begin to feel the energy of a project when you assemble for that first location scout. Maybe it's just the change of pace from all the reading, but you sense that something tangible is finally happening. Concept meetings, as often as not, are a part of these location van excursions. It's one of the few times when you have the director's uninterrupted attention, excluding, of course, the calls on the ubiquitous mobile telephone and the inevitable debate over where to have lunch.

Among those usually present on these early scouts are the director, the producer, the art director, the production manager, the assistant director, the location manager, and the transportation coordinator. The director rightfully expects to be shown only those locations with whom contact has been made and which will be available for filming. He also expects to have two or more choices for each location. Be sure to voice your preferences. You are responsible for the look of the piece, and location selection is critical to the film's ambiance. Very often, the director will find everything he wants at a location except for a few necessary elements. The needed changes might even be at your suggestion. This is where your contingency allowance for unexpected work pays off.

The producer, if he has lived with this project for a while, might well have such an engraved image of the story's locale that anything short of his ideal setting will be a disappointment. Be sure that you have his input as well as the director's when you start sifting through the early location selections. The producer will generally bow to the director's choice of locations.

The production manager is looking at the locations with an entirely different focus than that of the art director. One of his first priorities when he was the only one on staff was to produce a budget for the film, and now he is looking at a reality that was only a number a few weeks ago. It's not surprising that he should be looking for ways to make that guess hold true. An experienced production manager will have anticipated the inevitable location shortcomings and considered them in his budget. Art directors bear the same responsibility when they prepare budgets before locations are selected.

The assistant director can be expected to have the production board with him to remind everyone which scenes are scheduled for each location and what if any additional work has to be accomplished on that location day. Also in the back of the assistant director's mind is ever-present concern for the possibility of rain on the day of shooting. He will be looking for a "cover" set nearby into which he can quickly move the company. As a last resort, they can pack up and move to a stage or a distant interior set, but during the survey is the time to keep an eye out for that sheltered alternative location.

Cover sets will be required in almost any part of the country and during any time of the year. In the best of circumstances, rain will start the night before shooting and show promise of continuing all the following day. In that case the cover set, often on a stage, will have been prepared the day before and will be ready for the change of schedule. The awkward scenario is when the cover set is a "practical" location and owners are not attuned to the shifting schedules of a film company. They, the owners, might find themselves living amid some pretty bizarre surroundings for days as the set goes unused. Dressed sets that are kept standing by "just for cover" can be subject to unfortunate redecorating if left unattended.

Rain or the threat thereof reminds me of the time I was on location when the sky started darkening just as we were within a few hours of finishing our scheduled shooting. The worried production manager had driven out to the set to assess the situation. A dutiful production assistant reported to him that, on his last contact with the bureau, the weather man gave them about an hour before the incoming storm was due to hit. The nervous production manager, ever the negotiator, urged the young runner to get back to the phone and "see if he will give us an hour and a half!"

The driver of the van for these preliminary surveys is most likely to be the transportation coordinator. When it looks like a location has become a likely candidate for the show, he can be seen wandering around the perimeter of the site, mentally parking his equipment and trying to visualize what his options are for keeping the generator truck away from the camera.

The location manager is one of the first hired on the production staff. The art director's rapport with the location manager must be established early. You probably will be spending a lot of time together driving through various unfamiliar neighborhoods and often touring some very bizarre locations. Make available to him the research that you and the director have discussed. Sketch, if necessary, the physical and architectural elements you are looking for. Sometimes it takes a little pep talk to steer him away from that location

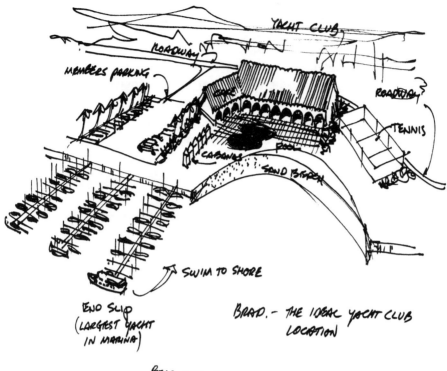

YACHT CLUB

ROADWAY

MEMBERS PARKING

ROADWAY

TENNIS

CABANAS

SAND BEACH

SWIM TO SHORE

END SLIP
(LARGEST YACHT
IN MARINA)

BRAD. - THE IDEAL YACHT CLUB
LOCATION

BRAD, LOOK FOR THESE
DETAILS FOR "INT.
DUDLEY MANSION"

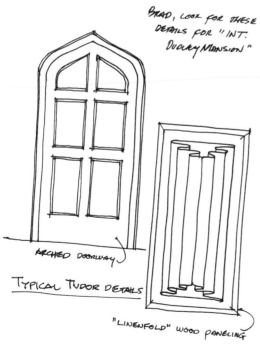

ARCHED DOORWAY

TYPICAL TUDOR DETAILS

"LINENFOLD" WOOD PANELING

The location manager will welcome even the briefest sketches defining your parameters for the ideal location. Architectural or decorative terms do not always bring to mind the same images. Sketches go a long way toward eliminating the semantic confusion.

he used on the last show, where parking was so convenient and permits were so easily obtained.

Location brokers are a phenomena that have developed in cities where filmmaking has become commonplace. Recognizing the market for movie locations and the unfamiliarity of most owners with the ways of film production, these entrepreneurs have contracted with the owners of many desirable locations to represent them in negotiations with film-production companies. Generally, location managers welcome the service they provide since these brokers usually have catalogued files complete with pictures and descriptions. However, don't let the convenience of this approach to location scouting lull you into the notion that you found the best possible location. It still takes a lot of old-fashioned leg-work to do the job right. And, of course, the expense of working through a broker has to be considered, even though the cost of location rentals is not a part of the art director's budget.

Preview each location with the location manager before showing it to the director. Do this not only to confirm that it is appropriate to the script and visual concept, but also to see that you're not imposing undue restrictions on the director by way of cramped quarters, unlightable areas, ambient noise, or delays caused by distances to the production vehicles. These production problems are the biggest killers of otherwise acceptable locations. With that said, I must point out that it is often the art director who has to make the argument in favor of a problem location. If you become a slave to the limitations of production problems, you might find yourself prematurely shutting the door on an exceptional location for which the director and producer are willing to make an extra effort for the sake of the added production value. No matter what location is finally selected, you can be sure that someone on the shooting crew will carp, "Who the . . . picked this location?"

For ***That Championship Season***, *the scenes filmed in Scranton, Pennsylvania, had to match those shot onstage in Hollywood. Photos taken during the survey make that possible.*

The inclusion of a ruler or an object of a known dimension in the photo is necessary if the set designer is expected to exactly reproduce the location setting.

It's not always possible to package a full day's work at each location. In fact, most shooting schedules end up with miscellaneous scenes that have to be included in days when you're shooting at locations not at all like what you would have hoped for. When a situation like this arises, it will soothe your damaged psyche if the term "compromise" is put out of your mind and replaced with the more acceptable concept called a "creative challenge."

Look next door, across the street, in other rooms. You will be surprised at what can be created from seemingly anomalous settings. Often this process of extemporizing will require the repainting of various portions of a location and the construction of some unusual set elements. These modifications should be explained to the owners since they are not usually accustomed to the movie industry's common practice of "instant remodeling."

Sequences that require the matching of actual locations with sets on a soundstage merit special attention when scouting. Architectural character, of course, must always be maintained, and when direct cuts are made from location to the stage (i.e., entrances or window POVs), every detail demands an exact match. Don't hinge the door on the wrong side or neglect to double-face the window unit. Photos and exact measurements are essential to this process. Standard survey paraphernalia should include: the script, your breakdown cards (showing scene numbers, etc.), a compass (where does the sun rise?), measuring tape, a boldly marked ruler to include in detail photos, note pad, camera, and more film than you really think you need.

Usually, stock backings can be found to match the character of common locations. If, however, the location is unique, or the backing becomes a significant element in the set, you will want to consider having photos taken at the actual location for a custom backing. As you will see in the chapter on special effects, projected photo transparencies or

*It was during the location survey for **Island Son** that it was decided to make custom backings showing downtown Honolulu and the state capitol building. A night version was also made. Photo: Courtesy of Color House PhotoBackgrounds.*

process projection plates may also be considered. While you are scouting for locations is the time to plan for these needs.

One of the things that proves most enlightening to location owners is the number of visits that they incur during the course of pre-production. If possible, try to brief them on the circus that follows: The location manager's initial contact usually comes a day or two after they notice strange cars prowling the neighborhood. He will take a lot of photos and then return with the art director, who will take more photos and do his own exploration. If the location survives the director's review of the photos in the office, the owners can expect the preliminary scouting party of the five or six mentioned earlier. This is sometimes followed by a second visit if the director wants to sort out the two or three finalists. Once the location is selected, the real parade begins: the location manager with contracts to sign; the art director with the set decorator, his lead man, and the construction coordinator; a construction and paint crew; the set dressing crew; and a final location survey just before the shooting date by representatives of the grip, electrical, and transportation departments.

Seldom, if ever, have I found the location that could be filmed with no preparation whatever. Don't take any location for granted. I nearly got burned a few years ago when I assumed that a Skid Row hotel room that was selected for its less-than-tidy appearance would be a simple drive-up-and-shoot location. On the afternoon before it was due to shoot,

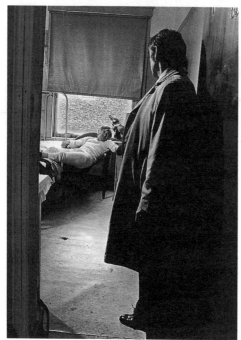

*In **The Stone Killer**, if Charles Bronson had shown up a day earlier, he would have found this suspect in a Skid Row room that has been freshly painted a bright turquoise blue. Photo: Courtesy of Columbia Pictures.*

I made my customary walk-through of the sets. The hotel resident of our perfect room had taken it upon himself to make the place more presentable for his "movie people" guests. He said he had gone on the wagon so he could afford to buy the can of paint needed to redecorate his room. Our returnee to the world of sobriety had no problem with his selection of hue, chroma, and tint. He explained that he simply picked his favorite color: turquoise blue.

Fortunately, I was able to contact my painter in time for him to come over and restore the room to its dilapidated grandeur with its water-stained walls and crackling paint as our now off-the-wagon host watched and wondered at the strange ways of them "movie people."

Design and Presentation

There's no business like show & tell business.

E very show, during pre-production, has most of us imagining limos, black ties, "and the winner is." These dreams are the icing on the creative cake and it's during the design phase of a project that these expectations glow their brightest. But the cake beneath the icing isn't too bad, either, when you consider the career of motion-picture design. It is the good fortune of motion-picture art directors to be the ones who are asked to bring to reality those images that each of us conjures as we read an exciting, romantic, horrific, or hilarious tale.

The first concept meetings should be as broad-based as possible, with the director being exposed to a wide variety of off-the-wall ideas. This is the time to open all the stops on creative brainstorming. However, once the director has settled on a theme or established a direction for the piece, the designer must shelve all those divergent ideas that he has been just dying to use. It pays to remember that the motion picture is a director's medium. All other creative contributors are just that: contributors. There will always be other shows where the concept of a color palette based on Pacific Northwest totem poles will be better received.

By the time there have been a half dozen concept meetings and location scouts, after the research sources have been
extensively mined and a ballpark budget is in hand, it's about
time to start designing. Unfortunately, that logical sequence
doesn't usually happen. Instead, production schedules often
dictate that set construction starts shortly after the art director comes on board. It's a good practice, therefore, to get into
the habit of sketching from day one. Even if the sketches are
way off target in terms of concept or budget, they are still
discussion tools—and in some cases might just be exactly
what the director had visualized.

The aesthetic and practical decisions that are made when
designing sets and locations require a background that can
best be described as eclectic. Bring to each project every bit
of experience you can muster, no matter how esoteric it may
seem at the time. A concept or idea that worked well on
another show or even in another career might just work here.
Without abandoning this concept of serendipity, let's now
explore the constants that will guide the design process.

Think and draw in a scale with which you are familiar.
Paper-napkin sketches are certainly helpful, but as soon as
possible, get into quarter-inch or eighth-inch scale (or metric
if that's what you're used to). It will be a leg up for your set
designer, and your visualization of the space will be much
truer. In elevation sketches, it is a good practice to include
human-scale figures to constantly remind yourself of the relative size of whatever you are designing. Don't get too cute
with these figures, however. I've heard of a whole presentation meeting falling apart when the discussion zeroed in on
why the guy in front of the saloon had a feather in his hat.

Preliminary design drawings will usually take on a life of
their own. Sometimes, the bare minimum of information is
all that is needed to inform the director of your intentions
and to start the set designers to work. On the project *Steel*,
however, it was a bit more complicated. The story centered

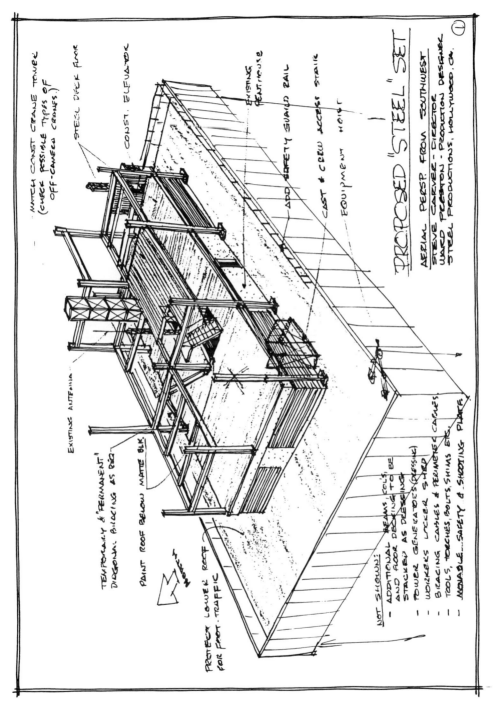

The sketch is labeled with the following handwritten notes:

- MATCH CONST CRANE TOWER (CHECK POSSIBLE TYPES OF OFF-CAMERA CRANES.)
- STEEL DECK FLOOR
- CONST. ELEVATOR
- EXISTING PENTHOUSE
- ADD SAFETY GUARD RAIL
- CAST & CREW ACCESS STAIR
- EQUIPMENT HOIST
- EXISTING ANTENNA
- TEMPORARILY & "PERMANENT" DIAGONAL BRACING AS REQ.
- PAINT ROOF BELOW MATTE BLK.
- NORTH
- PROTECT LOWER ROOF FOR FOOT-TRAFFIC

PROPOSED "STEEL" SET

AERIAL PERSP. FROM SOUTHWEST
STEVE CARVER - DIRECTOR
WARD PRESTON - PRODUCTION DESIGNER
STEEL PRODUCTIONS, HOLLYWOOD, CA.

NOT SHOWN:
- ADDITIONAL BEAMS, COLS, AND FLOOR DECKING TO BE STACKED AS DRESSING
- TOWER GENERATORS (DRESSING)
- WORKERS LOCKER SHED
- BRACING CABLES & PERIMETER CABLES
- TOOLS, TORCHES, BOLTS, SHIMS ETC.
- MOVABLE SAFETY & SHOOTING PLATF.

Preliminary design drawings sometimes find their way into pre-production meetings. Casual notes often stimulate detailed discussions of production problems.

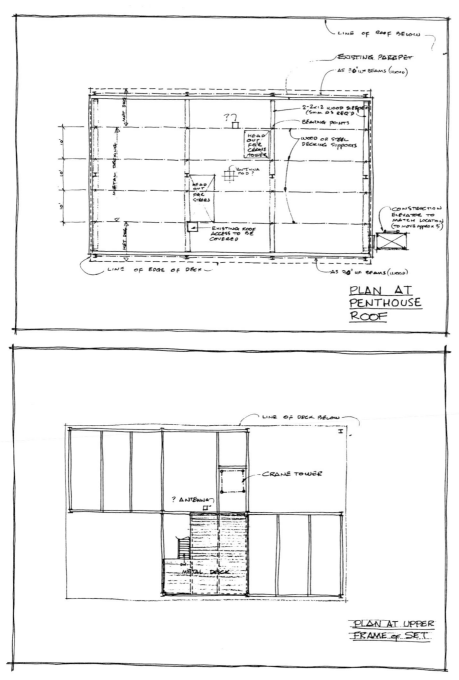

PLAN AT
PENTHOUSE
ROOF

PLAN AT UPPER
FRAME of SET

Plan views at different levels are necessary when there is a significant change in the set's configuration. Rarely is a second-floor set actually built above the stage level.

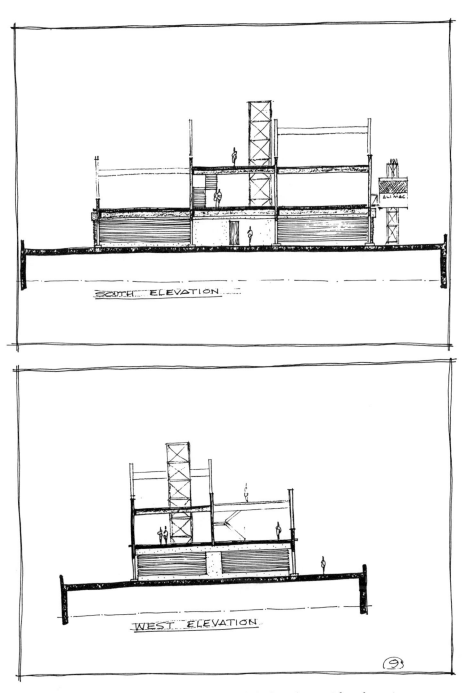

SOUTH ELEVATION

WEST ELEVATION

(9)

*Elevation views provide the most "natural" look at the set. Often these views
are colored and rendered in lieu of a full-fledged perspective illustration.
Scale figures are helpful.*

on a high-rise building under construction. Since we only had access for filming on the weekends, it was necessary to build a replica of the upper framework atop another building where we could film for the remainder of the week

Before construction could begin on this "set in the sky," it was critical that the director, the assistant director, the production office, and the art department be in full agreement as to which sequences shoot at which location and in what time frame. Meanwhile, the real building was changing every day and was rapidly nearing completion. Consequently, the preliminary drawings for this set were reviewed in many pre-production meetings. By the time the working drawings were drawn, if you will pardon the pun, most of the "nuts and bolts" problems of filming this set had been solved.

Continuity sketches, or "story-boards" as they are also called, are handy at this stage of a project. They can be an indispensable asset to a director or they can be an intimidating nuisance. Don't make the mistake of presuming that a director will jump at the chance to bring on a continuity artist. The director is not there to make the film as it is visualized by the art director or the continuity artist. It is only when the sketch artist becomes an extension of the director's imagination that the storyboard is valuable. If the director is prepared to spend the time necessary to imbue the artist with his thoughts and then critique and revise the sketches, then those drawings can indeed become the pictures worth a thousand words.

A seldom-used but valuable tool for reviewing the visual pacing of a film is a color-continuity strip. It can be up to eight-feet long, but need be no higher than four to six inches. This strip, which expresses the changing moods of the story can be made even before the general palette for the show is set. The strip corresponds in length to the total duration of the show. Using the script page count as a rough estimate of screen time, the strip is divided into the various sequences.

Using color and texture only, delineate the strip with the appropriate moods. If nothing else, it's a good starting point for discussions with the director on the "look" of the picture.

The real test of a designer's work is the story that the sets and locations tell. Let's hope that it's the same story that's emerging from the dialog, the action, the editing, and the score. And like the editing, the camera work, and the score, the sets are most effective when they don't call attention to themselves or overpower the story. Just as a composer can use tempo to induce tension or a minor key to convey sadness, the designer has in his vocabulary the visual tools to induce emotions. It is the designer's ability to manipulate visual associations that sets the style of a well-designed film. Lets examine these tools.

The warming and chilling effects of **color** are generally understood and accepted. Consider also the effects of the saturation or depravity of color or the absence of an entire segment of the color spectrum. There are times when black-and-white or monochromatic images can be more effective than the proverbial rainbow. Colors also carry with them the aura of their origins. Terms such as "sky blue" and "forest green" are obvious, but there are also many other color connotations—such as the royalty of purple, the refinement of white, the evil of black, and the baseness of scarlet—that can be brought into play. These emotional associations constitute a universal language that can be exploited by the sensitive designer.

Line and **form** make up everything we see and touch. Learn to exploit the sensuality of the curve, the abrasiveness of acute angles, the rigidity of a grid, and the freedom implied by flowing lines. Terms such as "breaking up" a surface or "softening" a line are almost universal among designers. The form that these decorative elements take when applied to buildings is often what determines their style or architectural period. The accepted way of establishing the period of

94-A

SALON IN SEMI-DARKNESS

FLICKERING LIGHT FROM OVER HEAD FIXTURES

RITTER WIND FAN

AS CAMERA ROLLS PEOPLE CLINGING TO FLOOR COME INTO FRAME

HI-SPEED WINCH FOR STUNT EXTRAS ON ~~WIRES~~ SHOCK CORDS

*A storyboard becomes mandatory when stunts and special effects dominate a scene. For **The Poseidon Adventure**, director Ronald Neame used production designer Bill Creber's team of continuity artists for planning the complicated sequence. Sketches courtesy of Dan Goozeé.*

SC. 108
TERRY (STUNT
ACTOR) FALLS

MASTER
ANGLE
SC. 106

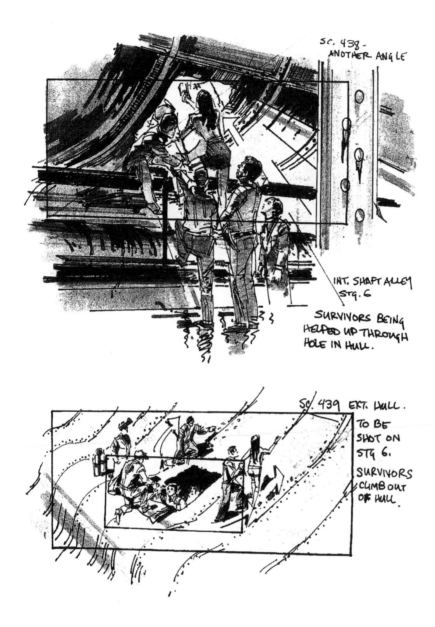

*Occasionally, "behind-the-scenes" sketches are necessary to supplement the conventional soryboard. Some elements of the rescue scene in **The Poseidon Adventure** were filmed next to the studio fence. Sketches courtesy of Dan Goozeé.*

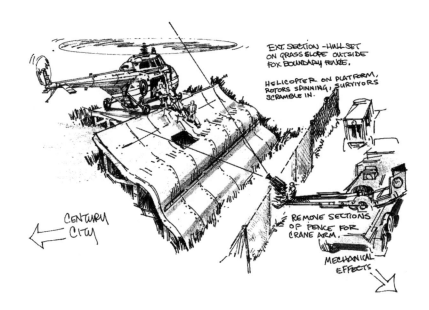

EXT. SECTION - HULL SET
ON GRASS SLOPE OUTSIDE
FOX BOUNDARY FENCE.

HELICOPTER ON PLATFORM,
ROTORS SPINNING, SURVIVORS
SCRAMBLE IN.

CENTURY
CITY

REMOVE SECTIONS
OF FENCE FOR
CRANE ARM.

MECHANICAL
EFFECTS

INT. SHAFT ALLEY
SET - STG. 6 -
ANGLE ON
HOLE IN HULL.
SCS. 436, 438

a frontier town is to adorn the porches, doorways, and windows with elements of Victorian ornamentation that connotes the origins of the inhabitants.

For the award-winning western *Unforgiven,* production designer Henry Bumstead wanted to reflect the harsh theme of the story in the design of the small town that was the setting for this tale of frontier injustice. Since the entire town was to be built from scratch, as opposed to modifying an existing western set, Bummy had a blank canvas with which to work. He consciously avoided using the decorative details that would give a degree of civility to this nearly lawless community.

Light and **shadow** are mainly the domain of the director of photography, but not entirely. Moldings since ancient times have been designed with shading and shadows in mind. The deep shadows of niches, colonnades and alcoves were architects' tools long before the first venetian blind was hung in front of an arc lamp. Set lighting, of course, can make or break a well-designed set. Be aware that flat lighting not only kills most textures but also diminishes painted aging. Cross lighting enhances textures, but it can also be a curse as it reveals blemishes and other imperfections. Sometimes, shadows are your friends.

Jack Collis, the production designer for *Far and Away* and *Splash,* remembers the days when his budgets were something less than generous. For a horror movie involving a cave-like crypt, he started the construction with a random wooden framework wrapped with flexible-metal stucco lath. The tight-fisted production manager apologized, but said Jack could only have one plasterer for one day to complete rock-like surfaces of the cave. To the astonishment of the studio plasterer, he was instructed to give his artistic touch of imitating rock striations only to those specific areas outlined by Jack on the walls. The rest was to be a conventional (and speedy) troweled finish. With the cooperation of the cameraman, the set was successful because wherever the walls were lit, they showed off the skillful work of that dismayed craftsman. Unseen in the shadows of the set were the not-so-convincing surfaces that the cameraman agreed to hide.

The term **texture** has been used to mean an indefinable quality of reality that lifts a film, a performance, or a setting out of the ordinary into the hallowed halls of filmmakers' Valhalla. In designer's terms, it has a more prosaic definition, but it can have just as much impact on a design. Textured walls take aging much better than flat walls. Textured floors are impossible to dolly across. When a texture is made orderly it becomes a pattern. Texture is much more than crackle paint and nail-riddled power poles.

For the movie version of the classic O. Henry short story *The Last Leaf,* Armitage Avenue in Chicago was selected to depict the turn-of-the-century Greenwich Village location. The elevated railway that crosses the street here is supported by very practical—but visually boring—plain steel columns. Using "texture" to help give this location the feeling implicit in a late Victorian artist's colony, I encased these columns in a lattice work simulating the riveted open-webbed strap-metal construction of that period. Further, the use of weathered awnings, extensive signs, exposed wiring, wet paving, and steam-shrouded street vendors completed the effect.

Why are the streets in movies always wet at night? Because when streets can be made to reflect light, they take on a more photogenic quality. **Sheen**, to the designer, is more than a legendary acting family. It is another tool to mold the character of a set. High-gloss paint gives an entirely different effect than the same color in flat paint. To some cinematographers, it's harder to light, while others welcome the "kicks" it produces.

In my first meetings with the director of photography on the pilot for a television series, he assured me that he was "not afraid of white" and that reflective surfaces were no

60.

EXT. PRAIRIE. BLACK BART RIDING ACROSS THE PRAIRIE DELLED OUT IN SPECTACULAR DUDS THE HORSE IS STEPPING OUT TASTEFULLY TO BIG BAD BEAT of the COUNT BASIE BAN

TIGHT ZOOM LENS.

THEY MOVE LIKE A MOIST DREAM.

CAMERA PANS WITH BART REVEALING PIANO

BOOM

This sequence from **Blazing Saddles** *(drawn by John Jensen) gave director Mel Brooks a preview of the bandstand layout that production designer Peter Wooley had planned.*

60 CONTINUED   CAMERA PANS WITH BLACKBART and SWINGS TO RIGHT ON

BOOM
ARM

REVEALING
COUNT
BASIE
and
ORCHESTRA
(THEY
APPEAR
TO BE
MOVING
BY
ACTION
OF
THE
CAMERA)

AS
CAMERA
PULLS
AWAY

BLACK
BART
EXITS
SHOT.

problem for him. After working with so many cameramen who were insistent on grayed whites and matte surfaces, this liberal philosophy was welcome indeed. Nonetheless, when we finally settled on the selection of the beautiful classic yacht to be featured in the show, I was sure that the mirror-like ceiling of the salon would have to be covered in one way or another. This inventive cinematographer not only "coped" with the unusual ceiling, he even featured it in several of his setups.

Understanding **kinetics** would seem to be a natural characteristic of a *motion* picture designer. Unfortunately, a lot of us hold to the "everything that doesn't move" theory and forget that we, as designers, are responsible for such animated elements as flashing signs, pendulum clocks, mobile sculpture, and flowing water. Sometimes it takes a little help from the special-effects man, but the rustling trees, the falling leaves, and the billowing lace curtains are also vital contributors to the images we create. And because motion does attract attention, kinetic objects should be perceived not only as dynamic design tools, but also as double-edged swords. Be aware of the attention they draw.

The other facet of the kinetic design is camera movement. Although designers don't have as much control over that aspect of filmmaking as the cinematographer, we can still provide them with the designed elements that make those moves most effective. Foreground columns, for instance, can enhance most dolly shots. Generally, interior posts and columns work to everyone's benefit except for the man who's working with the microphone boom. Set-dressing elements are equally effective as foreground pieces, and they can be "placed to camera" for the best composition.

Filmmakers often use **contrasts** as a storytelling tool, i.e., the Prince and the Pauper or the Priest and the Killer. Designers can also use the concept of contrast to emphasize such things as brightness, size, confinement, or opulence. That

Visualizing a set exactly as the camera will see it is the purpose of a set illustration. Artist Gary Meyer notes that here the fore-ground chair was intentionally diminished when it obscured too much of the set.

Preliminary studies in the form of sepia prints allowed illustrator Peg McClelland to try various color overlays. A thorough knowledge of perspective drawing is essential.

A color continuity strip is a good starting point for concept meetings. This strip abstractly represents a murder mystery which takes place in seedy locales, an upbeat art gallery, and concludes in an underwater search for treasure.

Illustrater Bill Majors' rendering of a snow-clad setting gives little warning of the menacing events about to take place there. These contrasts can make a horror story that much more vivid.

Rendering techniques may differ from show to show, but should remain consistent through the various sets on the same film. As shown here and above, Peg McClellan's use of raw pastel and Art Deco forms work well together.

Although the perspective layout may dictate the inclusion of off-camera elements, it is advisable to render the scene in the same aspect ratio (screen proportion) as the release print.

The gritty reality of an Appalachian coal mining town may not be apparent to the wide angle lens. As the story unfolds, the irony of this almost idyllic establishing shot becomes evident.

Seldom is it possible, but it is always desirable to combine the presentation drawings of the art director with those of the costume designer. This combination took a lot of coordination.

Grand Ballroom will seem a lot grander if entered from a vestibule rather than from the great outdoors. Intentional anachronisms can be used to convey a story point. A television set in an Indian hogan is as effective as a half page of dialog.

Equally effective as contrast is the concept of **placement**. Elevation connotes superiority, holiness, isolation, chilliness, and vulnerability while depression implies security, warmth, inferiority, and evil. The desk of a cunning executive might well be placed on a slightly raised platform, immediately putting his visitors at a disadvantage. Or, to give added intimacy to that recessed hearth-side inglenook, it can be placed a few steps below the level of the rest of the room.

Finally, it is as important for the physical environment of a story to have a history as it is for an actor to recognize his or her persona in the role. Even if it's never outlined in the script, and even if it isn't obvious in the final print, each setting should be designed considering the conditions and events that created that setting. Usually, it's necessary for the designer to invent this history for himself. Don't let this excursion into fantasizing scare you. In many ways, it's the most enjoyable phase of the design process.

Imagine that the storefront campaign headquarters for the candidate is in a building built in 1928 as a commercial investment by a developer who loses everything in the stock market crash of '29. His first tenant is a hardware store and they build a perimeter mezzanine to gain additional sales space and a small office. In 1944, upon the death of his son in World War II, the bereaved owner sells out to an inept manager, who runs the business into bankruptcy within two years. The owner of the men's clothing store who takes over in 1947 not only gives the façade a post-war face lift, but also installs dressing rooms and work space for a couple of tailors. A new shopping mall built on the outskirts of town in the '60s prompts the clothing store to follow the move from the downtown business district.

The space sits empty for three years. A dry cleaner, seeing the opportunity to use the cheap space for both his customer-service area and his cleaning plant, moves into the store. He installs dry-cleaning machines, a steam boiler, presses, and a motorized clothes-hanger rail running up into the mezzanine. The popularity of wash-and-wear clothes causes the cleaner's demise and, without totally stripping the space, it is repainted and occupied by a health-food store, complete with shelves, refrigerator, and a small deli-type eating area. Nutrisharama closes in 1978, so the space is available for the 1980 senatorial campaign of our hero. Armed with this scenario, a designer is much better prepared to make consistent decisions on design details, color, aging, and set dressing.

Presentation meetings are the art director's showcase. In preparing for these meetings, it pays to remember that the audience for a design presentation consists of show-business professionals. Give them all the glitz you can muster. Use models whenever possible and mood lighting if possible. It wouldn't be out of the question to play a John Philip Sousa march as you explained how the headquarters building was strategically placed across the parade ground from the barracks. A periscope viewer is also helpful in bringing the eye level down to the scale of the model.

Illustrations and continuity sketches are most effective if they are unveiled. Keep a fly leaf over each board until you are ready to present it. The colors and textures depicted in an illustration are often enhanced if accompanied by swatches or samples of the actual material. When it is appropriate, include the research photos in the presentation. It is no secret that these designs are the result of many hours of careful study. We're not trying fool anyone into believing that these ideas miraculously emerged as the result of a designer's orgiastic moment of artistic epiphany.

Location detail photos and panorama shots are as much a part of the presentation as the art work. Don't make the mistake of duplicating the work of the location manager. For speed and convenience of filing, his photos are most often Scotch taped together and folded into convenient manila folders. Give the art-department location photos the same respect we give to any picture. Cut, trim, and dry-mount your photos on artist's illustration boards.

Producer Don Klune reminds me that art directors might do well to follow the example set by our ex-boss, the late producer and master showman Irwin Allen. Adjacent to his office/conference room was his presentation room. When hyping a current project, let's say *The Poseidon Adventure,* he would conclude his opening speech by opening a curtain on the wall behind him to reveal a magnificent illustration of the luxury liner being capsized by a gargantuan tidal wave. Before the group could catch it's breath, he ushered them into the presentation room, closing the door to immerse them in the world of drawings and models depicting the hapless travelers' trek through the inverted world of a doomed ship.

While they were in the presentation room, Donald, the office aide would replace the rendering in the office with another and close the curtain. When Irwin thought he had wrung out the last ounce of amazement from his guests, he would take them back into the office for a concluding pitch. The punctuation to this wrap-up would have many thinking that Irwin had forgotten his timing as he once again dramatically opened the curtain. However, this time it revealed the chaos in the Grand Salon at the moment of the spectacular disaster. *That* is a presentation!

With today's easy accessibility of video cameras and VCRs, it is possible to juxtapose models and illustrations with video shots made on location scouts. Short of providing a buffet lunch and tap-dancing magicians, there are still plenty of manipulations that can be used to spice up a design presentation. It is interesting to speculate what an Irwin Allen presentation would be like today, given the tools of our current technology.

Set Construction
"We don't plan to build any sets."

I t is the production manager's heart speaking rather than his head when he says, "We don't plan to build any sets for this show." As surely as he would plan for rain in Seattle, he really knows that set construction of some kind is going to be needed on all but the most basic of documentary shows. Even on a so-called no-set show, try to anticipate those inevitable preparations that are needed on every location. Painting, greens, signs, interior alterations and off-camera construction such as safety barriers are what come immediately to mind. Location construction and the use of local resources will be covered in later chapters.

Set construction on a soundstage is the meat and potatoes of art direction. The film industry's years of experience with this system has resulted in the closest thing that Hollywood has to an assembly line operation. When compared with the confusion and frustration of building sets on location in a warehouse with semi-trained personnel, working in a full studio facility is almost like a holiday. Consider the various shops and departments at the disposal of the art director:

The **Mill** not only has every power woodworking tool imaginable, but also has floor layout space large enough to

The mill is the largest of the backlot shops. Usually, sets are built on the stage with the mill space being reserved for such construction as door, window, and fireplace units. Photo: Courtesy of Warner Bros. Studios.

pre-assemble all but the largest sets. The lumber and molding racks would put many lumber yards to shame. And if the exact molding you need isn't on hand, they have shaper machines that can run more. Indeed, if the profile isn't the right configuration, new knives can be ground to your specifications. The lathe man can produce anything from balusters and porch posts to Civil War cannons.

If you are a stickler for reality, you could have that same cannon made by the **Metal Shop.** Lathes, mills, sheet-metal shapers, and foundry facilities are basic fare for this valuable studio shop. The metal shop is often near its second cousin, that house of wizardry called the **Prop Shop.** As the name implies, they can make anything from a poison-concealing locket to a 30-foot replica of the Queen Mary. As often as not, the prop shop is also in the repair business. Making antique sewing machines or Victorian automatons workable would not be unusual requests.

The **Special Effects** department has overlapping needs with the prop shop and often shares facilities. For instance, the prop shop will build the consoles for a mission control center, and the special-effects team then brings them to life. The frequent appearance of computer images in film scenes has created a new special-effects technician: a computer programmer who can stand by on the set to operate the various monitors. He also can usually provide the special TV electronics necessary to prevent "banding" on the picture tube. Unique to this department is the casting of breakaway glass. Explosive storage and handling, of course, is done in special licensed facilities. Today, special-effects technicians are usually separate contractors operating out of shops apart from the studios.

No, the **Staff Shop** isn't where the supervisors hang out. Staff is a plaster of Paris material with a fibrous binder that came into existence when the designers of the temporary

The staff or plaster shop is an architectural treasure trove. Once a casting is made of a wall surface, a statue, or a complex molding, they can turn out as many duplicates as you can afford. Photo: Courtesy of Warner Bros. Studios.

buildings for the first World Expositions were seeking a substitute for cut-stone ornamentation. It's derivation is generally attributed to an old German word *staffieren*: to fill out or trim. Some people feel more comfortable calling it the "plaster shop." If the staff shop is given a prototype model, they can cast duplicates of almost anything. And, if you don't have a prototype, they will bring in a modeler or sculptor to make one.

The earliest of the backlot streets used staff "skins" to imitate the exterior surfaces of brick or stone buildings. Because of the weight of plaster, these skins today are molded in fiberglass, foam rubber, or vacuum-formed plastic. The development of resins for castings has also put the staff shop in the foundry business. Hardware door escutcheons, raised letters, and ornamental hinges are common requests.

Now is probably the time to mention the **Hardware Department.** Pilferage on motion-picture sets has not usually been a problem. However, if any single category of items can be regarded as in jeopardy, it's the hardware. For some reason, these items are considered fair game to those of a felonious nature. Of course, there'll be some surprised vandals when the brass paint comes off those plastic resin key plates. It's a blessing that the imitations are available. Gathering enough matching hardware to complete a large set would be next to impossible without them. The hardware department normally has its own technician who will install and remove all the locksets, bolts and latches. This is also the place where you'll find metal numerals for doors, mail slots, door bells, and bath accessories.

For the bathroom fixtures themselves, and the many other plumbing devices that are needed to complete a realistic set, visit the wonderful world of the **Plumbing Department.** I am always amazed at the diversity of plumbing fixtures that a studio assembles over a period of time. Aside from the obvious residential facilities, I've also run across railroad and shipboard wash basins, steam radiators (both real and lightweight), European one-pass water heaters, restaurant dishwashers, and a stainless-steel therapeutic whirlpool bath.

Even though it is more often the domain of the set decorator, the art director will become a regular visitor of the **Electrical Fixture Department.** Giant crystal chandeliers, street lamps, neon signs, bracket wall lights, and, strangely, gas-fired medieval wall torches adorn this exotic warehouse. They also have wall switches and electric outlets appropriate to most eras and countries. By the way, for a long time the head of this department at Fox Studios was Bill Ryan. He stayed on and continued to efficiently run the fixture shop there even after his brother-in-law, Richard Nixon, became the president of the United States. As they say, "There's no business like show business."

While we're at it, we might as well pay tribute to the other venues claimed by the set decorator, but always toured by the art director. Each studio has a **Property House**, but I doubt if any show has ever been dressed out of a single house. Some prop houses are known for their specialties, such as weapons, electronics, or hand props. Don't visit a prop house when you're on a limited time schedule. You'll never make up for the time you've spent browsing.

The **Drapery Department** is not only a lifesaver when you have to hide a wall on location, but a good drapery man can suggest window treatments that might not have occurred to you. Once, when asking the name of the drapery man, he replied that I could call him "Rags." I went into a long discourse on how creative it was that he should pick such an appropriate nickname. No, he said, it was short for his Swedish name, Ragnar.

Often drawing from the same fabric resources as the drapery department is the **Upholstery Shop**. Whether it's an occasional pillow or the emperor's sedan chair, this shop has probably already done a dozen similar projects. Before committing to an entire seating group in an exciting material, it will pay to have a short meeting with the costume designer. It would be a shame to see our actress disappear in the inadvertent camouflage of similar colors.

Prior to getting that new upholstery, the decorator can check the piece into the **Furniture Refinishing Shop**. Sometimes this is just another function of the paint shop or it can be a separate shop. In any case, it's unlike any commercial shop in that they also have perfected the art of aging and weathering pieces as the story may dictate.

The arts of aging, texturing, and creating faux surfaces make the studio **Paint Shop** the creative center of the backlot. When showing my concern over the way a wood replica of an iron fence was being assembled, I was reminded of the art director's first commandment: *All the camera sees is the last coat of paint*. With that in mind, the importance of this critical craft comes into focus. Painters actually put in very little shop time. The spray booth is here and the color mixer, but most of their work is on the stage or location.

The painters are also the source of some of the best backlot stories in the industry. My favorite is the one about the master set painter Ronnie Kropf, who was in the wrong place at the wrong time. While working alone one night painting a nearly completed set, he was confronted by the show's producer. "This door isn't in the right place," he barked. Ronnie, although vainly trying to explain his limited duties was, nevertheless, coerced into accompanying the producer on a tour of the set as he cited numerous physical changes that had to be made. When the producer concluded his unexpected walk-through and was about to leave the stage, this talented painter, by now feeling a closer bond with the executive, left him with the reassuring valediction: "Don't worry, sir. We'll get this set right if it takes every nickel you've got!"

Painted backings seem to have lost favor in deference to the translucent photographic backings. However, there are

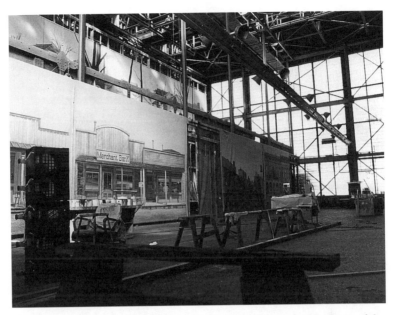

Scenic artists can be found to do everything from reproductions of the old masters to trompe l'oeil painted backings. Note the huge movable frame in the scenic loft shown here. Photo: Courtesy of J.C. Backings.

still some **Scenic Backing Lofts** in existence. Most have gone into the backing-rental business, and their inventory includes a mixture of painted as well as photo backings. A studio for this operation is unique in that it requires a space for a movable vertical frame that might be as large as 30 feet high and 150 feet wide. To keep every portion of this huge "canvas" within reach of the artist, the frame is capable of being raised or lowered through a slot in the floor into a room below the studio.

The job of hanging the backings, whether painted or photographic, accrues to the studio grips. Not to be confused with the company grips, these crews operate out of the **Grip Room** and are responsible for striking sets, hanging overhead-light scaffolding, moving stock units to and from the stages, and installing muslin ceilings—as well as hanging backings.

The final studio resource I'll mention and one of the most vital is the **Sign Shop**. They service the decorator and property master as well as the art director (not to mention executives' parking-space signs), so you can seldom find a more overworked crew. Most now include computer-generated signs as well as silk-screen and hand-lettering options. One of the most difficult types of signs to have made is the amateur "protest sign." A professional sign writer, even with film-studio experience, has a difficult time corrupting his work enough to make it look amateurish. Do these signs yourself or turn them over to a production assistant.

Once you are familiar with all the backup a studio facility has to offer, it's time to start work onstage. A **Soundstage** designed for set construction will have many advantages over a converted warehouse, i.e., ample electricity to operate power tools, compressed-air outlets for sprayers and tools, running water and sinks for paint crews, level wood floors suitable for nailing, removable sections of flooring over pits into which staircases can descend, an accessible, reinforced overhead grid from which to hang light scaffolding, heating and air conditioning units, and, of course, proper sound insulation.

Another commandment: *Be there when it's still just lines on the floor.* This is your only chance to make adjustments before they become costly changes and morale killers. Is there a fire-access area around the perimeter? Is there room to maneuver a backing into position? Is the pit in the position you planned for? Does the space "feel" the size you thought it would? Does it just miss aligning with an overhead support? Are there any unexpected conditions (a floor sump, an uneven floor, overhead obstructions)? When you're satisfied that all is well, get off the stage. Work will go a lot faster in your absence. I don't know why, it just does. Another mystery of the backlot is that no matter when you plan to visit the stage, the foreman will have called a coffee break two minutes before you got there.

For what it's worth, I'll pass along a universal theory of working crews. In every group of five to fifteen workers brought together to perform a given task, there will be one or two who far exceed your expectations. They will do more work, have better attitudes, and take more pride in their work than the others. On that same crew will be one or two laggards. The rest fall somewhere between these extremes and will do effective work if properly encouraged. The obvious question: Why not lay off the laggard and hope to hire another go-getter? Experience has shown that when the new man comes on, if he is a self-starter, he may go to the top of the heap, but one of the top performers will slip into the middle group. In the meantime, the laggard slot will be filled by one of the marginal members of the crew. You're really no better off than before and you have taken a chance of hiring the type who can sour a whole crew, the trouble-maker.

Unique to the field of set construction is the concept of removable or "wild" walls. Once a scene has been rehearsed and the camera moves have been established, it's time for that frantic period of motion-picture production called set lighting. It's time for the grip crew to display its efficiency at transforming a painstakingly reproduced Mid-Victorian drawing room into a shambles of lamps, grip stands, gobos, cables, and dolly track. To accomplish this feat of planned chaos, it is necessary that certain walls be specified as wild walls.

Most walls or construction units can be removed by simply pulling some special double-headed nails or by backing off on a few strategically placed screws. Other units such as backbars or bookcases may require caster wheels and counter-balancing weights. Only rarely are walls or units "flown," as is the practice for stage scenery. One imaginable situation would be when an interior wall is otherwise locked in by joining walls. The potential hazard of lifting such a heavy object, even though counter-weighted, over the heads of a working crew cannot be ignored, and every possible safety measure should be observed.

The selection of walls to be made wild is based on a visualization of the stage during filming. If you will imagine the camera, the crew, and the lamps in place for each setup, the wild walls become obvious. When the wilding of certain walls is inhibited by physical problems, be sure that the director is aware of any limitations this may present. Also, remember that each of these wild units must be moved quickly, easily, and by sheer muscle power. Therefore, heavy, double-faced walls and lengthy pieces, should be avoided, and wilding joints should fall in logical places that can be easily patched.

Ceilings were almost nonexistent in the early days of filmmaking. Early set-lighting techniques dictated not only an absence of ceilings, but also required overhead platforms or scaffolding. When sets were so large that the camera could see over the top of the already exaggerated high walls, "headers" were used. Headers are false beams that cross between the camera and the back of the set, thereby screening the top of the back wall from view. A view down a hotel corridor set is a good example of multiple headers as one header screens another and the illusion of an unseen ceiling is maintained.

As filming became more sophisticated, removable ceilings were introduced to give directors the latitude of more natural camera angles. Very often, these ceilings were only muslin fabric pulled taut across the opening between headers. With the change to lower illumination levels, the technical advances in compact equipment for tight location shooting, and the practice of lighting from the stage floor, it is not uncommon to see sets today with hard ceilings that may or may not be removable for lighting.

Where lighting techniques do require overhead lamps, whether on manned scaffolding or movable rigging (light bars), sets must be designed accordingly. Indeed, there are times when the location of existing scaffolding (also called parallels, light beds, or green beds) dictates the layout of the set. For some television and three-camera shows, entire walls must hinge out of the way for set changes and relighting.

Most of the problems of simulating reality on a studio stage have long since been resolved using conventional construction techniques and processes. A brick wall may not really be a brick wall, but it definitely looks like one. The single greatest dilemma for art directors has always been and continues to be, "How do I make what is seen through the windows believable?" The choices are many, but most are something less than satisfactory.

Building the set on an actual location, of course, is the best way to provide believable backings, but short of that, it may be possible to position the set on a soundstage, taking advantage of a stage door for a view to the natural exterior. Or, studio backlots often have space enough behind the false façades to build an interior set. These solutions compromise the control of sound, daylight, and weather inherent in closed-stage work, but the tradeoff is often worth it.

When the window of a stage set is presumed to look out to a light-well or to a nearby building, full-sized walls including doors and windows are effective backings. Forced-perspective backings with miniature buildings can work in a situation where the camera position is predictable and makes no drastic moves from that spot. Rooftop and penthouse terrace sets demand a combination of backing systems if the illusion is to be complete. A cyclorama of 180 degrees or more is basic to this kind of set. The horizon, if not painted or photographed on the cyc, is represented by a cut-out profile. Intermediate objects or buildings are depicted in various miniature scales.

Painted scenic backings have definite limitations, but one of their advantages over a photo backing is that an entirely different backing is not necessary when changing from a day to a night sequence. Many painted backings are selectively opaqued on the backside. When lit from the rear, windows come alive and a city-glow emanates from the horizon. For daytime use, they are their most effective when seen through the diffusion of a scrim that is lit to give the effect of a natural haze. Of course, dirty windows, blinds, or sheer curtains always help, too.

Backlit photo transparencies have become quite good and will be found in the catalogs of most of the backing rental houses. The older photo backings are colorized by hand-tinting, and because time has brought about many changes in the subject matter, some are not reshootable. The state of the art for color transparent photo murals is at a point where almost unlimited sizes can be produced. Custom color houses exist where you can order backings photographed and printed to the specific needs of the set.

Rarely used for window backings, but still available, are rear-projection screens. The problems are the space needed to operate the slide or motion-picture projector and keeping ambient light off of the screen surface. The advantages are the easy changeover from dawn to day to dusk to night, or in the case of "process" projection, incorporating movement into the background. Another option for backgrounds in motion is by way of the "blue screen" optical effect to be discussed in a later chapter. All of these processes place severe limitations on camera movement and, therefore, should not be considered until they have been fully discussed with the director and the cinematographer.

The greatest pitfall for any backing scheme is a misplaced horizon. It is an optical fact that the line of the horizon is always at the level of the observer's eye, Whether standing on the beach or looking from the rooftop restaurant of the beach-front hotel, the horizon will appear to be level with your eyeline. If seated in the restaurant, the horizon will appear in one window pane. When you rise, the horizon will

◉ BACKINGS CORPORATION

451

20 X 15

450

25 X 18

453

30 X 15

452

25 X 18

Painted backings are available for most types of settings and often are "opaqued" to work for both day and night. Some backgrounds are impossible to create by way of photographs. Photo: Courtesy of J.C. Backings Corp.

appear to rise with you to the pane above. Controlling the position of a backing as the camera level changes is obviously impossible. Determine the most common height of the camera lens off the stage floor and set the backing horizon to match. When a clear horizon is not obvious, find the place on the backing where horizontal lines on buildings are truly horizontal. There are usually two or three extra feet of backing on the bottom of the roll when the horizon is properly set. That's as it should be.

There will be times when the extra backing at the bottom of the roll will come into play. Occasionally, when the view is critical and the window-sill line is unusually low, the set must be built on a raised platform. Imagine a high-rise executive suite with floor-to-ceiling glass. In an exaggerated situation such as this, it will probably take more than two or three extra feet of backing to complete the desired illusion.

Building sets on platforms, by the way, introduces some significant production problems, not the least of which is sound-deadening the construction to prevent squeaks and drum-heading. All the production gear, especially the camera dolly, must be repeatedly lifted into place, and special movable work platforms must be built to be placed next to the elevated set. There are production managers who would rather chew tinfoil than approve a set to be built on a platform.

With the preponderance of independent productions today, it's worthwhile mentioning here the set-construction resources available to the art director working on a project without the backup of a studio facility. If the project is based in the Southern California area, you have the advantage of being within range of many of the one-time major studios. Most of them are now in the facility-rental business. If your production offices and soundstages are off the studio lot, you still can make use of their property houses, staff shops, mills, and sign shops on a purchase or rental basis. Backlot streets are commonly rented by independent productions.

16' 4" x 40' 10"

Chromatrans CT-217

16' 4" x 40' 10"

Chromatrans CT-218

A-3 LA

Colored photographic backings are usually back-lit and come in matching day and night versions. Avoid seeing such areas as city streets where movement would be expected. Photo: Courtesy of Pacific Studios.

Shooting on a studio backlot allows the kind of control that filmmakers must sacrifice on location. There is often enough space behind the façades to build interior sets as well. Photo: Courtesy of Universal Studios.

Directories specializing in film-related businesses are available in most major cities through the local film commission. And of course, the old reliable yellow pages are always there for the builders' supplies, nurseries, antique shops, paint stores, sign writers, wallpaper and floor-covering specialists. The relationships established with these vendors will be very much like those noted in the chapter on distant locations.

Finally, a word about plants and landscaping. The effectiveness of greens as a softening element has been well established. When the nature of a show dictates the presence of a full-time greensperson, take advantage of this talented technician. A thoughtful placement of appropriate greens just outside a critical window will enhance most backings and the most mundane residential streets can come to life with the presence of colorful, scattered leaves. A last word of advice: When live plants are used on a stage, provisions must be made to ensure their periodic sunning and watering. Drooping greens can kill a mood faster than a speck of broccoli on the leading man's dentures.

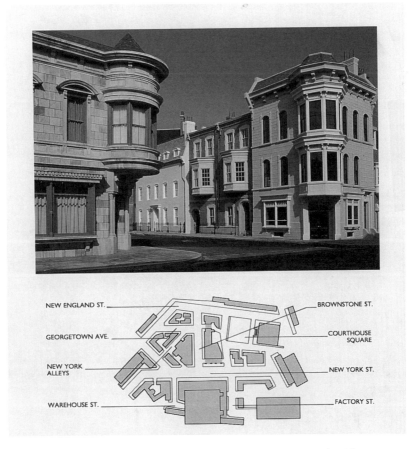

NEW ENGLAND ST.

GEORGETOWN AVE.

NEW YORK ALLEYS

WAREHOUSE ST.

BROWNSTONE ST.

COURTHOUSE SQUARE

NEW YORK ST.

FACTORY ST.

Rental streets on studio backlots are available in many styles. The rarity of these vestiges of the major-studio system is making them all the more valuable today. Photo: Courtesy of Universal Studios.

Set Decoration

"I thought you had the punch bowl."

If an art director were to be judged on just one decision he makes during the course of a show, the most telling would be his choice for set decorator. It has taken the Motion Picture Academy a number of steps to recognize the contribution of the set decorator. Until 1941, there was no category for this demanding job. From then until 1947, a certificate was awarded to the decorator of the film winning the art-direction award. From 1947 through 1954, this recognition was upgraded to a plaque. Since 1955, identical Oscar statuettes are given to the art director and the set decorator for the film winning the Art Direction Award.

The furnishing and detailing of a movie set is unlike any other kind of interior decoration. In fact, one of the cruelest criticisms of a set is that it looks "decoratorish." It's worth remembering that we are, above all, involved in telling a story and that real life is not always color-coordinated with blemish-free furnishings. A successfully dressed set or location should become as much a part of the actor's persona as the clothes on his back. I've heard the argument presented that a fully dressed, four-walled set is not an extravagance, even though half of it never gets on film. The director who made this case said that actors who have the opportunity to browse and rehearse in a total environment will give better performances. Indeed, their reaction to a prop or some unexpected item of set dressing might just inspire a "bit of business" to improve the scene.

For *Purple Rain*, the dressing room in the nightclub sequences was built on a stage. I designed it to look like it had been converted from a bus drivers' locker room. (The 1st Avenue Club in Minneapolis was, in fact, a remodeled bus depot.) The decorator, Anne McCulley, had her work cut out for her in layering the room with decorative elements as Prince and his troupe would have done to take the curse off of this grungy setting. Along with the assorted posters, wardrobe, and makeup accessories, she included toys and collectibles that the entertainers would have cherished. The pop-up doll that Prince casually handled during rehearsal became a significant hand-prop in the show.

The matter of "props," by the way, brings up one of the more common sources of conflict on any show. The set decorator and the property master have overlapping areas of responsibility. If they are not constantly communicating, some very embarrassing duplications or omissions can occur. Consider the wedding reception where the decorator has coordinated the decorations and table settings. The food, drinks, and caterer are the domain of the property master. Let's hope that the decorator and propmaster anticipated this sequence with a lengthy meeting. Or, imagine the possibility of the deceased wife's picture in our hero's wallet not matching the framed photo of her on the desk. Most property masters savor their autonomy, but if they can be diplomatically persuaded to maintain a close tie with the art department, these problems can be avoided.

It is normal for the art director, the set decorator, and the decorator's crew to stand by for the first setup in a new set or location. Efficient scheduling precludes their standing by

The practice of taking "set stills" complete with slated identification has disappeared. A full-time still photographer made sure that he shot each set before it was torn apart.

*Rental property houses offer the widest range of styles and character imagin-
able. Whether making an historical epic or a space-age fantasy, you'll find
the basics in a prop house. Photo: Courtesy of Universal Studios.*

for the full day's shooting. Therefore, after the inevitable adjustments for staging have been made, the removal and replacement of the set dressing falls into the hands of the property master, his assistant, and, depending on the scope of the set, whatever additional on-set dressers may be needed. Once again, communication with the property master is vital if the intentions of the set decorator and art director are to be followed up during shooting. It might be that one of this crew could be encouraged to take those desirable set stills while they're taking their customary Polaroid continuity shots.

The set decorator's crew includes a lead man, a set-dressing crew of three or four, and a driver or two. Often, the drivers can be counted on as helpful members of the set-dressing crew. Once out of sight of their Teamster brothers, they have been known to bend the rules and lend a hand. With the demands of pick-ups, drop-offs, dressing, striking, and packing, they are the most mobile group on the show. It's a good idea to provide this crew with mobile communication in case a change of schedule should require their attention.

Frantic changeovers and last-minute panics are bound to occur, but in the normal scheduling of set preparation, always allow the decorator and his crew enough time to properly dress the set. Let the construction coordinator and especially the paint boss know that their deadline is well ahead of the date on the shooting schedule. Large sets may take up to a week to properly dress, and it can't be done around sawhorses and wet paint. It is only fair that the decorator should have the necessary time to experiment, add aging, and generally fuss over a complicated set. Keep the painter available to do the final aging as it is suggested by furniture and fixture placement.

The final noodling in the dressing of a set can be the most exasperating and the most rewarding phase of the design

The set decorator, when encouraged to reach out for that extra something, can come up with some very exotic artifacts. Museum-quality pieces are sometimes the results. Photo: Courtesy of Warner Bros.

process. At this stage of the game, you have worked closely with the decorator in getting to this crucial phase. You have looked at all the research together and have probably seen most of the dressing. Now, let the decorator and his crew have a free hand as much as possible. Once the set is roughed-in and the basic arrangement agreed upon, review it with the decorator and decide what help he can use from the construction or painting crews. Incidental shelves, broken stair rails, exposed electrical wiring, and plumbing cut-outs come to mind as last-minute chores.

To be sure that there are no gaps in responsibility for completing the set, an early decision should be reached as to what areas are covered by whom. The following guidelines are subject to change, but in general they are recognized as standard practice.

The art director's construction crew should provide:

Hardware for doors, windows, and built-in cabinets
Door numbers, sign plaques, and hanging signs

Wallpapers, veneers, and built-in shelves
Windows, stained glass, and glass blocks
Plumbing fixtures, including radiators and water heaters
Built-in kitchen appliances
Vent grills, exposed ducts, and pipes
Hard flooring and sometimes wall-to-wall carpeting
Awnings, entrance canopies, and large tents
Greens (when in a "natural" state)
Billboards, marquees, and fixed electrical or neon signs

The set decorator's dressing crew should provide:

Incidental hardware: wall hooks, bathroom accessories
Drapery hardware, blinds, and valances
Interior shutters on windows
Area carpets and sometimes wall-to-wall carpeting
Light fixtures, switches, and electrical outlets
Exposed telephone wire and "wiremold"
Posters, lobbycards, desk signs, and hanging neon signs
Campers' tents, temporary canopies (wedding or funeral)
Interior and potted greens.

Of course, all of these items are covered in discussions between the art director and the decorator. Many of them, such as carpeting, wallpaper, light fixtures, and built-in appliances are selected on joint visits to the appropriate suppliers. Ideally, the talents of the set decorator and the art director will mesh to produce a result better than either of them might have originally envisioned. It should be their mutual challenge to present to the director more than he expects, or, as it's known in the South, *Lagniappe*: "a little something extra."

The most critical of any of the art director's presentations is the final walk-through of the set with the set decorator, the director, and the producer. Be sure that all of the light fixtures are wired and working. If possible, have the gaffer send someone to the stage to temporarily light any window backings. Be creative in the mood you establish with the

When preparing a set for the walk-through with the director, make every effort to have all the lights working and the scenic backings properly lit. It may be the last time you see it this way.

props and dressing. Have the hero's smoking pipe and iced cocktail beside his favorite chair. Have his dress uniform laid out on the bed. Turn on the stereo and have coffee brewing in the kitchen.

On the classic western *Monte Walsh*, the decorator was Phil Abramson, doing one of his first shows. He had the good fortune to have production designer Albert Brenner as his mentor. Phil was eager to convey the ambiance of a cowhands' mess hall that was run by a ranch cook, who the script noted to be a less-than-fastidious housekeeper. Two weeks before the walk-through, Al suggested that Phil place a slab of raw meat in the fly-infested barn. Just before the presentation, as he was adjusting the grimy array of pots and utensils, Phil opened the jar of putrid meat and hid it beneath the chopping block. When director Bill Fraker reacted to the offensive odor during the walk-through, he complimented the team on their inventiveness and suggested that they perform the same bit of olfactory legerdemain when the actors showed up on the set.

Distant Locations

Starting from square one.

F ilms requiring distant-location work have existed since the embryonic days of the motion-picture industry. Although early filmmakers are known to have traveled widely to explore the capabilities of this wonderful new toy, they sometimes found it easier to recreate a street or jungle on a backlot rather than to move a film company to the actual site. Admittedly, these early creations were pretty poor substitutions for reality, but the so-called backlots expanded and thrived. By the time of the major-studio era, the detailed replicas of European streets, Oriental temples, and Mississippi river boats had become quite sophisticated.

It takes a substantial organization to maintain a backlot and to use it often enough to make it economically viable. The dissolution of the major-studio system sounded the death knell of extensive backlot filming and introduced the era of runaway production. The high costs of local work with union crews and the growing availability of trained technicians at distant locations plus the incentives offered by state sponsored film commissions lured filmmakers to the far reaches of this country and even into Canada. Today, location filming is the norm rather than the exception.

The first few visits to a potential location are usually made by a scouting party consisting of the director, the producer, the production manager, and the art director. Guided by representatives of the local film commission, they are shown not only the appropriate locations for the script, but also local restaurants, hotels and points of interest. While there, the scouting party is treated like visiting royalty, given such perks as complementary hotel suites and access to the governor's plane for aerial scouting tours. Not only does a film production company make a significant financial impact on a community, but there are considerable residual benefits from the tourist trade generated by a successful film.

When the decision is made to film at the desired location, a production office is established, often in the hotel where the cast and crew will be housed. The art director then decides where he can best set up an art department. Usually, this is in office space near the production office. The space should be large enough for the art director, an assistant art director, an illustrator, a set designer and, an art-department coordinator (Girl Friday). The set decorator and construction coordinator should also have office space close to the art director. The director's office should be nearby for pre-production meetings. This is not as important after shooting has begun, because then meetings will usually be held on the stage or in the director's motorhome on location.

The challenges to the art department are quite different when the entire production is based on location. Facilities that are taken for granted back in the environs of a working studio must now be found here on location. Tasks such as renting office furniture and installing telephones can be handled by the production office, but it is up to the art department to find drafting equipment, art supplies, a blueprint shop, and a one-hour photo service.

One of the first facilities thath must be found is an industrial space or a warehouse that can be used as a set-construction shop. Often, the need for a soundstage as well as a workshop would seem to dictate that they occupy the same building. This can work very well as long as there are no conflicts between the shooting schedule and the demands of construction. Not only is there the obvious problem of noise, but consider also the effects of dust on the set dressing and the offensive aspects of paint fumes.

When setting up the workshop space, the art director should review it carefully with the construction coordinator. Is there enough power capacity for the anticipated rental tools and compressors? Are there drains and water supply for the painter? Is there enough layout space to pre-build set pieces? A resourceful construction team, when left to their own devices, will soon solve the problems of racks for lumber storage, office space for the plan table, and a nook for the coffee setup.

Another sizable space is usually needed for the storage of set dressing. Even when a show is dressed entirely with rented furniture, there are bound to be purchases and items on hold that will require a storage area. When the set decorator finds this space, he will need the help of the construction crew to build an enclosed area within this space for the lockup of valuable dressing and props. He will sometimes set up his office in this "gold room."

The space to be used as a soundstage should be evaluated on many levels: Because it probably is not sound insulated and because the cost of installing sound insulation is prohibitive, the location of the building should be as far removed from noise sources as possible. The clear space between columns must be large enough to accommodate the planned sets. The clear ceiling height must allow for the tallest set plus another eight feet or so when scaffolding for lighting is called for. If suspended scaffolding is planned, verify the ability of the roof trusses or girders to take the load. When the floor is concrete and therefore not nailable, a decision must be made whether to tie sets down with sandbags and braces or to install a plywood overlayment in the set area. Consider heating or cooling the stage when extreme climates are anticipated. For the safety of the crew, verify that fire exits will be adequate when the sets are completed. As was noted for the workshop, the stage will need power, water, etc., during the construction phase.

For the film *UHF,* producer Gray Fredrickson described to the Oklahoma film commissioners his ideal location. They were able to find, in one location, a facility that provided us with a soundstage, a construction shop, property storage, production offices, an art department, and living quarters for the crew, all under one roof, and fully air-conditioned. On the outskirts of Tulsa was a newly finished shopping center/office building/hotel complex that was a year or so ahead of its time. A couple of unfinished stores in the mall gave us excellent stage and construction space. A full floor on the eight-story office tower was more than ample for our production offices and art department. And we could walk to work in air-conditioned comfort from the connecting highrise hotel. I would hope that the spectator activity created there by the film company's work was the boost needed to get that enterprise off the ground.

On a couple of distant locations, I've made use of professional house movers. When faced with the challenge of creating an entire rustic town on a scenic bayou near Uncertain, Texas (yes, that's really its name), I contacted the owners of abandoned homes and sheds in the area and bought the unsightly relics. I even bought the abandoned post office for the town of Karnak, Texas. Doyle Ross, a nearby housemover, transported and spotted these ruins adjacent to the picturesque waterway as I directed him, much like placing furniture in an empty room. Doyle later admitted wondering about the quality of my judgment in these novel purchases. With the help of some add-on modifications, store-front façades, a boardwalk, and waterfront pier, it made a very believable Cajun village. It has been used by other film companies since then and was a local tourist attraction for a time.

Incidentally, it wasn't too long after this project that the same house mover (by now attuned to my unusual requests) was able to bail me out of a sticky location situation. I needed a depot to be positioned alongside an existing steam railway line. A small residence in the adjacent town was in the final stages of being refurbished when I proposed to the owner that we borrow his house long enough to move it to the rail line and dress it as the town depot. Once he stopped laughing and realized I was serious, he tentatively agreed to the arrangement. However, by the time we got around to signing a contract confirming the details of our agreement, he apparently had received some lawyerly advise, because the clauses were expanding, the price was escalating, and I was climbing the walls.

When I told my plight to Doyle, whom I had standing by to move this house, he offered to sell us one of the small houses he had in his storage yard some hundred miles away from there. Days later, when we went back to cancel our negotiations with the gold-digging owner, it was with some satisfaction that we were able to point at the new depot being lowered into place. It worked out much better because, owning the building, I was able to add a telegrapher's bay and extend a bracketed overhang.

The art director's search for local craftsmen and suppliers is best done in the company of the construction coordinator. One of the most important technicians is the sign writer. A town of any size at all will have a couple of sign shops. Most sign writers welcome the challenge of matching an historical period or creating already-weathered signs. The problem is impressing a sign-shop owner, who probably has an established clientele, with the do-or-die deadlines of

The backroads of East Texas proved to be the mother lode of resources for the creation of a waterfront Cajun village. These shacks were purchased and moved to the new site.

The town of Soggy Bottom takes shape as the recycled shacks undergo an architectural face-lift. The painters, for once, are given a head-start in the aging process.

With the exception of a "new" bank building, each store was a remodeled building.
With a new bayou setting, the old post office became the sheriff's office and jail.

a film company. This job and that of the paint boss are best handled by studio-trained craftsmen, especially when extensive aging or character work is anticipated.

Before opening charge accounts at the various material-supply houses, the construction coordinator must make sure that they understand the accelerated pace of his building program. For example, when working on an overnight revamp schedule, it might be necessary to have after-hours access to a building-supply store. Or, it is not uncommon, when time is of the essence, to have a film company truck and crew pick up wallpaper or carpeting directly from the store's supplier. Most lumber yards, paint stores, and flooring suppliers will gladly accommodate the special demands of a film company.

Thanks to his pre-production foresight, production designer Norman Baron was able to able to deliver an almost instant set when the emergency arose. It was midday when the director realized that his campsite setting in the forests of North Carolina would be unshootable on the following evening because of impending rain. Given the challenge of reproducing the campsite, Norm rallied local equipment companies and personnel whom he had briefed on the possibility of last-minute work. His enthusiastic gang flew into action: A warehouse/stage was rented. Some 20 tons of dirt and boulders were delivered. With the daylight hours waning, they harvested the remains of full-grown trees that were scattered in a nearby woods as the remnants of hurricane Hugo.

Working through the night, they erected tree trunks on stands, created trees from limbs and brush, strategically placed some boulders, and wrapped the set with a night-black backing. The set was ready in less than 24 hours for the following day's shooting. Norm not only won the director's admiration, but also caused himself a problem: With miracles now commonplace, it was only a week later that the

*The dramatic concluding sequemce of the film **Steel** involved a team of helicopters "topping out" a high-rise building. Only with the complete cooperation of the city of Lexington, Kentucky, was this possible.*

director asked for (and got) an instant river! But that's another story.

It usually takes a week or so for the owners of equipment-rental yards to get the smiles off their faces when they hear that a movie company is coming to town. Unless your construction coordinator has his own tools, compressors, and generators, etc., these yards will thrive during your stay. Production managers understand this situation and will usually pay a weekly rental to the construction coordinator who brings his own gear. You can still anticipate that considerable expense will be involved in the of hiring local contractors and the renting of miscellaneous construction equipment. It's worth it to hire the pros.

For the Lee Majors high-rise adventure story *Steel*, we found a site that enabled us to build our set atop a 17-story building in Lexington, Kentucky. Fortunately, we were only a few miles from one of the largest heavy-equipment movers in the state. Watching construction equipment and material being lifted 200 feet or so by a ground-mounted crane is an impressive sight. In a move to minimize the cost of this operation, a motorized over-the-edge davit arm was built on the roof to do the work of the crane. It worked very well until the shooting company was evacuating the roof during a thunder storm. While lowering the crab dolly, the braking mechanism got wet and failed, sending the dolly into a 150-foot free fall in which it buried itself in the concrete plaza, narrowly missing the crew member holding the tagline below. The savings quickly evaporated.

The most elusive local resource is that of a "scene dock," or a place where the art director can find "stock units." On location, that translates to a building salvage yard. These enterprises can vary from an upscale operation with multiple stories devoted to mantels, stained glass, and carved doors (as I saw in Chicago), to the humble backyard of an eccentric pack rat. This search often overlaps with that of the set decorator's quest for local thrift shops. The one-man operations sometime introduce into negotiations an element unknown in commercial establishments—an emotional attachment to their product.

On the comedy feature *Soggy Bottom USA*, I accompanied the set decorator, Bob Zilliox, as we frantically tried to locate a weathered wooden-duck decoy. It was near the end of the day when we found, in a little rural town outside of Marshall, Texas, a long-forgotten store that was now occupied by a world-class pack rat. The sign in the window proclaimed that this stuffed-to-the-ceiling maze of junk was an "Antique Shop." In that very same window was a very old, very weathered, wooden-duck decoy.

Not wanting to seem too anxious, Bob and I browsed for a while before Bob casually asked the cigar-smoking proprietor if, among other things, he might have any old wooden ducks. "Nope," was the old man's considered answer. After vainly trying to finesse an admission from the owner that he did, in fact, have a decoy for sale, Bob finally blurted out in desperation that he had an urgent need for that duck on display in the window and would pay any price for it. "Oh, I can't let ya have that one, son," apologized the colorful owner, "it's the last one I got." Our quest for an old wooden duck was extended for another full day.

Special Effects

From squibs to mattes to morphs

O ne of the first images that comes to mind when special effects are mentioned is that of a huge explosion. Although this is one of the more spectacular results of a "special effect," it is only one phase of the "movie magic" with which art directors are expected to be familiar. Most special effects require the art department's direct participation, and the visual aspects of all special effects are the art director's responsibility. From bullet hits to blue screen, it's all part of the *enhancement of communication by visual means.*

Generally, special effects can be divided into two basic categories: physical effects and optical effects. They require the talents of two very different kinds of practitioners. The standby special-effects man may be called upon to: water down a street for night filming; create smoke, fog, rain, wind, or snow; make and trigger bullet hits, explosions, and fire; collapse a ladder, release a spill tank, or "fly" an actor (usually a stunt double) by wires. Most stunts require the assistance of the effects department. Breakaway props, windows, and railings, car rollover mortars and ramps as well as barricades and safety nets fall within the purview of this multi-talented mechanic.

It's the physical effects that are of the most immediate concern of the art department. When the script calls for action in a shower, cooking on a stove, or a fire in a fireplace, the set construction must be adaptable to these so-called "practical" applications. Designs and continuity sketches of action requiring breakaway sets or explosions need to be discussed during the critical period of pre-production. Usually, "doubles" or multiple replacements of window frames or set pieces with exploding bullet hits (squibs) are needed so that they can be used for "takes" two, three, or four. Care must be taken in designing these breakaway units to facilitate their rapid replacement. Reloading while the company waits is time running on a very expensive meter.

Physical special effects also pose the greatest potential danger of any of the activities in which the art director will be involved. Don't make the mistake of assuming that because preparations for a dangerous stunt or explosion are in the knowing hands of professionals, they are therefore destined for success. If necessary, take the position as the coordinator of the destruction of that architectural masterpiece of yours. Did the man placing the explosive mortars know which beams were balsa and which were pine? Were any of the fire-resistant gypsum walls violated to run propane lines? Make sure that you give the assistant director, the effects coordinator, and the stunt coordinator a thorough briefing on the geography of the location (especially at night) and verify that they are all working toward the same goal that the director invisions.

For the film *Porky's Revenge*, production designer Peter Wooley built a replica of a paddle-wheeled river boat, complete with an operating casino. The climactic demise of this ornate beauty was the shearing off of the upper level by a drawbridge that refused to open. You can imagine the coordination necessary for this effect. Not only did the cable-assisted collapse of the upper decks have to be per-

*The gambling boat in **Porky's Revenge** is looking its glitzy best just before the ill-fated last cruise. Below, the top deck is wiped clean by a drawbridge that refuses to open. Photo: Courtesy of Robert A. de Stolfe.*

fectly timed and the crap-shooting cast protected from the havoc above, but the vertical tolerance was so close that the scene had to be scheduled for the last minutes of an outgoing low tide! Peter reassured the operators of the bridge that the calamitous spectacle posed no real threat to their structure. The shot came off perfectly. The only unplanned expense was for $75 to replace a lamp that hung beneath the span.

The other side of the movie-magic coin is the field of optical or photo effects. Today's wizardry in this area is expanding at an almost incomprehensible rate. However, to better understand the process, let's explore the whole range of effects, some of which are now rare if not extinct.

The term "matte-shot" refers to the matte-black cutouts, which, when placed in front of a camera lens or in contact with film being printed, prevent the emulsion from being

*This sequence from **Won Ton Ton, the Dog Who Saved Hollywood** involved a studio tour bus that got too close to a carnival set during a hoodlum bombing. The Culver City Studios used for this filming was actually the site for many silent films. Photo: Courtesy of Paramount Pictures.*

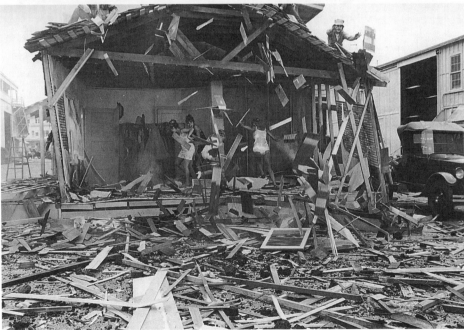

In this "one-take" sequence [top], it was important that the stunt coordinator be fully briefed on the physical preparation of the set. Can walls be scaled? Which props were breakaway? The shot showing the effect on the dressing rooms [bottom] just after the blast was, in fact, filmed much later to allow for the designed "destruction" of the set. Shingles are tossed from off-camera. Photos: Courtesy of Paramount Pictures.

exposed, thereby saving that portion for the later exposure to a different image. An early example of the double-exposure and use of camera mattes for special effects is in Georges Méliès pioneer science-fiction film *A Trip to the Moon* of 1902. It is certainly crude by today's standards, but extremely sophisticated considering the infancy of the medium.

The "in-the-camera" optical effect was further developed in the early days of filmmaking when the background was made to appear in motion by way of an image projected on the rear of a translucent screen that was placed behind the actors. Most commonly called a "process" shot, this photo-effects procedure is still in use today as a backing for automobile or railway mock-ups. The camera and the projector must be interlocked to assure that the shutters of each are opening at the same rate and at the same time. The stage space required for the long projector "throw" can sometimes be controlled by the use of a large mirror.

A variation on the rear-projection process is the front-projection system, which was made possible by the development of a highly reflective projection screen. Instead of placing a projector behind a translucent screen, the screen is replaced with a super reflective surface, and the projector is mounted next to the camera. By an arrangement of mirrors, the axis of the projected image is made to closely match that of the camera lens. Although you would expect to see the projected image on the clothes of the actors and on the walls of the set, the low intensity of the projector lamp coupled with super reflectivity of the screen results in an effect that is not apparent on the stage, but is easily visible through the camera lens. The Introvision Studios have successfully combined live action with still slides, miniatures, and multiple projectors to make this a versatile modern version of in-the-camera special effects.

With all the advances in the field of compositing multiple images, it is still often necessary to introduce into a filmed sequence a picture that can be created in no other way than by an artist's painting. This introduces the work of "matte paintings" by "matte artists." Artist Sid Dutton of the Illusion Arts Company describes his work as follows:

"There are two different techniques used to create matte-painting composites. In both methods, the live action is photographed first. Care must be given to tailoring the lighting so that it will correspond with the proposed matte painting.

"In one method, the live action is projected on a screen placed behind a painting done on glass. The clear portion of the glass allows the live action to show through while the painting itself mattes out the unwanted areas of the frame. When photographed together, the result is a convincing composite of the two images.

"With the second technique, the matte painting is photographed on the same film that was used for the live action, eliminating the re-photographing of a projected image as described above. To accomplish this, at the time of live action photography, a cutout black cardboard matte is placed in front of the camera, obscuring the area that will be represented by the matte painting. Therefore, when the live action is filmed, the matted area remains unexposed. Only enough of this film is developed to give the artist a single frame from which to work. The rest is held unprocessed with its latent image while the artist creates the painted image. He limits his painting to only the area defined as unexposed on that single frame. With the painted image complete, the remainder of the frame area is made matte black. Now the painting is aligned and photographed on the original film stock realistically blending the two images."

The process described above raises the question, "What about a scene that requires the live action to overlap the matte line?" When the encroachment is of short duration as in the case of a horse rider's head momentarily rising above the matte line or perhaps a balloon rising into the sky, each

The first stage of a matte painting is to expose a few feet of film, revealing the undoctored image—in this case, a commercial airline hanger at LAX.

The foreground and background action is then photographed with the matte in place. The actors are directed to not cross over the matte line.

After the space shuttle is painted to exactly match the angle and perspective of the shot, it is composited by exposing the film this second time to only the painted image. Photos: Courtesy of Illusion Arts.

The matte painting of the space shuttle is done at a convenient size, working with a projected image of the hanger interior. It must be confined to the area of unexposed film.

With the painting carefully lit and positioned to align with the partially photographed image, the studio camera exposes the remainder of the film. Photo: Courtesy of Illusion Arts.

affected frame can be treated separately with the matted area changing position from frame to frame or "traveling." Needless to say, custom matting frame-by-frame (rotoscoping) is not very cost-effective if an entire sequence requires this individual attention. It was only with the introduction of digital electronic matting that this type of traveling matte became practical at all.

The more common need for a traveling matte is when it is impossible or impractical to place the actors in life-threatening or fantasy situations, such as in a fatal fall or maneuvering a galaxy starship. When all or most of the background has to be invented, a traveling matte can be created in the film developing lab by a process known as "blue screen." It gets its name from the intensely lit, vivid-blue background against which the foreground action is filmed. By a special process of film developing, a single color (in this case, bright blue) can be identified on the negative and completely erased. The negative with a "hole punched in it" is then used to produce a very accurate traveling matte. Disney Studios, in their early productions combining live action with animated characters, developed a "sodium-screen" system that worked on the same principle but didn't produce a blue "halo" that sometimes occurred around the foreground character.

The counterpart of the blue-screen system in the electronic world of television is called chroma-key. The principles are quite different, but the results are the same, and most impressively, the marriage of the different images is immediate. This kind of television special effect is now taken for granted and used regularly on the daily-news broadcasts and on other live presentations such as sports coverage. I don't intend to get involved the field of television special effects, but it's hard to avoid the merging fields of optical and electronic imaging. Chroma-key was only the beginning of the revolution.

With television commercials setting the pace, photo or

Death-defying stunts can now be filmed with traveling harnesses and support cables in place, knowing that they are removable from the final print through digital retouching. Photo: Courtesy of Pacific Data Images.

The perennial problem of assembling (and holding) huge crowds for a motion-picture sequence has been solved by the digital technique of "copying and pasting" smaller groups. Photo: Courtesy of Pacific Data Images.

optical effects are advancing in quantum leaps. The budgets for filmed commercials in terms of cost per minute of screen time are astronomic compared to those of feature films. Therefore, it's not surprising to see these advertising marvels at the leading edge of the effects revolution. The constant expansion of computer technology now makes the frame-by-frame approach to filmmaking practical. Not only does this apply to the animator's art, but more importantly, in the mind of the motion-picture art director, it allows the retouching, if you will, of filmed sequences. For instance, stunts requiring cables or wires to assist the effect may now be photographed with the knowledge that those give-away lines can be removed from the print.

The creative people at Pacific Data Images recently took on what might be considered the greatest challenge of their impressive history: trying to explain to me, a computer dunce, the workings of their digital magic. Simply speaking, the strip of film to be doctored is scanned, frame-by-frame, into the computer's memory where, as digital information, it can be manipulated by talented computer programmers. Those offending cables can be "brushed" out, images can be "cut-and-pasted," and the relationship of each frame to the next can be controlled for the perfect blending of continuous motion. When the desired goal is reached, the digital information is transferred back into the medium of film with no loss in the resolution from the original. In fact, in special cases, the image can be made to appear sharper!

Of special interest to those art directors who may find themselves involved in the fantasy genre is the computer specialist's ability to transform ("morph") an object or person from one state of being to another. The original screen version of Lon Chaney, Jr., becoming the Wolf Man pales by comparison with today's illusions.

Computers and the Future

Are we ready for virtual reality?

T he process of projecting a focused beam of light
through a series of transparent pictures at the rate of
20 or so pictures per second originated over 100 years
ago. At the time, the concept of animating photographs to
give the illusion of motion was looked upon as a frivolous
invention that, at best, could be included as a side-show attraction at the latest world exposition. Without really straying
too far from that basic system of projection, the motion-picture industry proceeded to become one of the most
influential of the communication media.

It is not until after World War II, with the advent of television, that this system of presenting pictures in motion is
challenged. And, what a difference. The action it presents is
in real time without the customary delay for developing.
Ironically, the early television systems cannot record their
transmissions and have to rely on filmed Kinescope prints
to preserve or rebroadcast their programs. The eventual development of magnetic tape recording finally severs
television's early dependence on the film medium.

As it turned out, television's strongest link with the movie
industry was hinted at with the popularity of the Hopalong

Cassidy reruns. Filmed series, movies made for television, and the purchases of classic film libraries are ample evidence of the symbiosis that has developed between these once-belligerent industries. The mixed media conglomeration that Hoppy's success really foretold was epitomized when Sony International acquired the Metro-Goldwyn-Mayer studios.

Computerized colorization of films has been met with mixed reactions, to say the least. My only contact with the process was during the early state of the art when we wanted to colorize some World War II newsreel footage to incorporate in the biographical film *Ike, the War Years*. The effort was moderately successful, but my lasting impression of that project was in a theory proposed by a film-lab technician. He suggested that if we could find the original camera-exposed negatives of these black and white films, it might be possible that they contain a latent color image! Even though the emulsion was designed to react to degrees of light or darkness, he theorized that the wavelength or color of the light was somehow buried in that emulsion as well. If this is possible, we probably have the computer capability today to unlock those long-hidden secrets.

Today's miracles of merging media make it possible to publish an encyclopedia that can be carried in your pocket on a compact disc, searched in a fraction of a second, and read on a computer screen. If the subject is Mozart, you can hear passages from any of his major works, or see a sequence from a film on his life. Interactive television makes it possible to alter the plot of a mystery story with the detective following the line of investigation suggested by the viewer. The future portends the transmission of everything from stereophonic sound to physical objects by way of invisible electro-magnetic waves. Even the last great hope of the light-projection process known as holography with it's potential for three-dimensional motion pictures will eventually find its way into the embrace of electronic imaging.

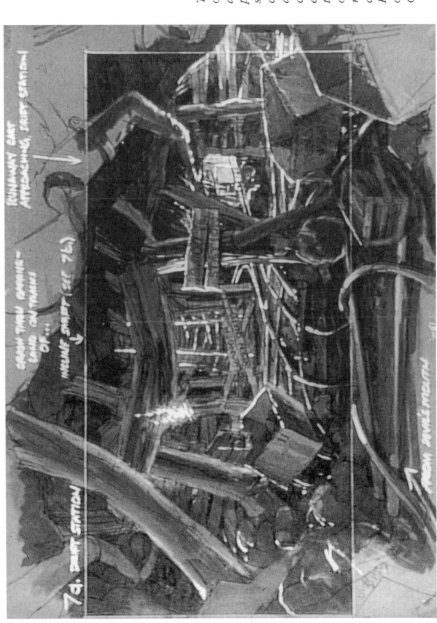

The precursors of virtual reality are motion-picture ride simulators. The challenge to designers is to create enviroments that often exist only in the memory of a computer. Photo: Courtesy of Showscan Corp.

Already, we can see the results of the computer revolution. Virtually every work station in every office focuses on the monitor of a main frame or personal computer. Typewriters have been replaced by word processors, and pinball machines have been superseded by video games based on mind-boggling software. Computer graphics and animation have advanced to the point where a car can be made to appear to change from a convertible to a formula racer before our eyes, and sophisticated prototypes have shown us that we are on the brink of having a personal environment simulator, which will appropriately be called Virtual Reality.

What does all this have to do with the price of shortbread in Savannah? Well, nothing. But it has everything to do with the design of environments for motion pictures. Art directors are going to be called upon to design more extensive and varied settings than ever before. The hitch is that many of them will never be built! They will only exist in the memory of a computer disk. It is not inconceivable that all of Caesar's Rome could be rebuilt and made available to visitors who subscribed to a Virtual Reality Travel Net. Those of an adventurous bent could experience the last days of Pompeii as members of VIRSA (Virtual Reality Survivors Anonymous).

Not only will this fantastic future world require ingenious hardware and software designers, it also will demand of the artists who design these computer images, a working knowledge of the medium. Just as artists coming into the world of film have to learn of camera angles and wild walls, the designer of the future will be expected to be familiar with pixels and baud rates. Computer Aided Design or CAD systems will be the easels and drafting boards of tomorrow, and now is the time to add the computer to the film designer's toolbox.

Most of the "film" schools, indeed, even the prestigious American Film Institute, recognize the overwhelming momentum of electronic imaging. Their bulletins and curricula are more and more reflecting the influence of television, com-

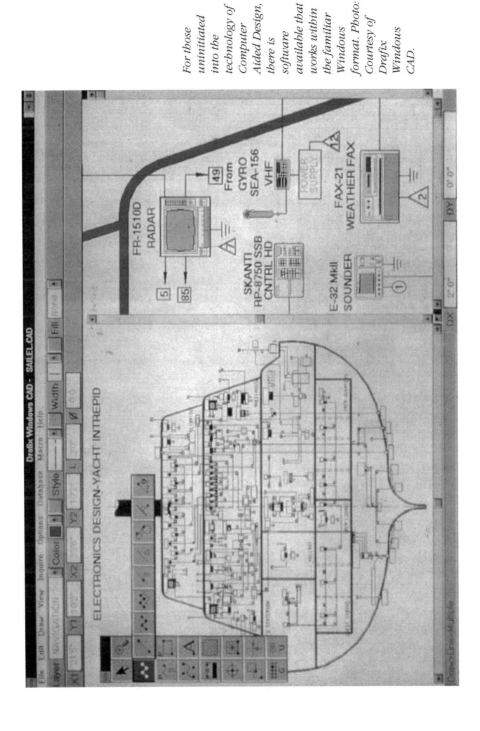

For those uninitiated into the technology of Computer Aided Design, there is software available that works within the familiar Windows format. Photo: Courtesy of Drafix Windows CAD.

puters, and digital systems on the motion-picture industry. Just as the VCR has made it possible for the film student to review an immense library of classic films, it also is opening the door to inexpensive experimentation in motion-picture techniques. This experience in electronic imaging will not be forgotten by the future generations of "filmmakers" (tapemakers?).

The current state of the art in computer technology gives art directors the opportunity to produce working drawings, lay out accurate perspective drawings from any conceivable camera angle, or take an animated ride through a proposed backlot street. The "wire frame" drawings of the early computer graphics are rapidly being improved to produce believable surfaces that are realistically textured, shaded, and highlighted. Just as assistant directors now rely on computerized breakdowns, as soundtracks are being recorded digitally, and as film editors are now commonly editing on tape, art directors should jump into the swim or at least sample the water of the twenty-first century.

Production Design

It don't mean a thing if it ain't got that *LOOK*.

I n an industry where the screen credit is as important as the pay, it's not surprising that so much effort is made to jockey for a better job description. Consider the many executives, managers, associates, writers, directors, and actors who covet the credit "Producer." Directors of Photography are still shaking off the currently passé appellation of Cinematographer and hoping that no one will recall their earliest credits as Cameramen. Once upon a time, Film Editors were Cutters, Set Decorators were Dressers, Production Coordinators were Secretaries, Transportation Coordinators were Driver Captains, Continuity Supervisors were Script Girls, Costumers were Wardrobe Men or Women, Lighting Technicians were Electricians, and Grips were, well, Grips.

The Art Department is certainly not immune from this quest for status. As was noted in a previous chapter, the title that best describes the work of an art director or production designer, i.e., Set Designer, was adopted long ago by the art-department draftsmen. Most Assistant Art Directors now merit the credit Art Director because the art director for whom they work has managed to garner the title Production Designer.

The credit Production Designer has been used in various ways: To recognize a job that goes beyond the responsibilities of art direction by also directing the work of the Costume Designer, the Property Master, the Makeup Artist and the Hair Stylist; Or to bring a designer of recognized ability from another discipline onto a picture where his or her motion-picture expertise is limited and it is therefore necessary to also have an Art Director on the show (sometimes this credit is Visual Consultant); Or to upgrade an Art Director when the scope of the show is such that it will call for an unusual effort and perhaps require the help of Assistant Art Directors who are deserving of the credit Art Director. Finally, it is too often the credit that is given to satisfy the ego of the art director while not adding to his staff or increasing his responsibilities. The title doesn't cost the producer any more money, and it upgrades his project to one worthy of a prestige credit.

Historically, the first art director to receive screen credit as a Production Designer was William Cameron Menzies for the masterpiece *Gone With The Wind*. Ironically, he was not eligible for an Oscar nomination because the Academy of Motion Picture Arts and Sciences did not at that time recognize the credit Production Designer. The Academy Award for Art Direction in 1939 went to Lyle Wheeler, who was the Art Director for *Gone With The Wind*. Realizing the inequity of bypassing Menzies on this technicality, the Academy created a Special Award and presented him with a plaque honoring his ". . . use of color for the enhancement of dramatic mood . . ." It is probably one of the least descriptive definitions of the job ever printed.

In the years to follow, the credit Production Designer comes into use more and more as a prestige credit, superior to that of Art Director, but the authority and responsibilities of the job are never really clearly defined. The Academy accepts the credit and places it, still without adequate definition, in the logical category of art direction. Currently, identical statuettes are awarded to the Production Designer, the Art Director, and the Set Decorator.

The elusive nature of the production designer's responsibility was evidenced in the mid '60s when the Broadway musical *My Fair Lady* found its way to the screen. To lure much-acclaimed costume designer Cecil Beaton onto the show, the film's producer granted him both the Production Designer and the Costume Designer credits. The picture deservedly went on to win the Oscars in both categories. The Art director on the show, Gene Allen, was of course recognized in the award, but he was responsible for far more of the creative effort on the film than the presumed secondary position would imply.

Whether the title is Production Designer or Art Director, it is still the responsibility of this artist to create a distinctive quality or a "Look" for the production. Sometimes this can be as simple as never seeing the color red on film. Other parameters can become so complicated as to require the full-time presence of the designer standing by the camera. The extent to which this hands-on approach to art direction is carried can either strain the designer's relationship with the Director of Photography or create a bond of mutual respect.

The process of production design is seldom confined to the selection of locations and the design of the settings. When a production designer is brought on early enough and has the respect of the writer, producer, and the director, it is possible for him or her to have a profound influence on the finished production.

In an early concept meeting on the film *Beguiled,* production designer Ted Haworth was told that the budget had to include the cost of staging a Civil War battle to run under the opening credits. Considering this to be an extraordinary expense that would constrict his already-strained set budget, Ted proceeded to do a storyboard that substituted the live action with a photo-montage of Civil War stills. He sold the producer and the director on the idea, thereby saving a considerable sum of money, some of which he was able to invest in the necessary authentic historical style. As a bonus, one of these old photos actually resembled the star, Clint Eastwood, as a young man.

The stylistic look of a production is one of the first decisions to be made and will be the subject of the earliest concept meetings. The best way to put a handle on the elusive concepts of aura, mood, or the quality of a show is to present the director with examples of an artist, an era, a design philosophy, or any visual material that can be discussed with tangible evidence at hand. Too often good ideas are lost or misinterpreted because of semantics. The popular buzzwords of "texture" and "layering" are of little help when their meanings have to be visualized in the mind's eye.

Films have been influenced by art movements since the birth of the medium. In 1921, the acclaimed *Cabinet of Dr. Caligari* imported the current European fascination with Surrealism as a design motif. The mono-monikered silent film siren Nazimova (no, Cher and Madonna aren't the first), when she starred in the 1922 production of *Salome,* languished in sets influenced by the erotic drawings of Aubry Beardsley. More recently, the depression-era work of Edward Hopper and the contrasting images of sensual blossoms with parched bones created by Georgia O'Keefe have found favor with designers seeking a handle on the "Look."

The following buzzwords have been heard in concept meetings for years and are sure to come around again. They are offered here as a springboard to young designers who are still honing the fine art of "Design Speak": John Singer Sergeant, Winslow Homer, Hudson River School, Thomas Eakins, Ashcan School, George Bellows, Robert Henri, Grant Wood, Pointillism, Seurat, Norman Rockwell, comic books, and the currently popular surrealist, Magritte.

Production designer Henry Bumstead maintained the '30s theme of The Sting *by having scenic artist Jaroslav Gebr paint the "act-change" cards in the style of the* Saturday Evening Post *covers. Photo: Courtesy of Universal Studios.*

The definitive description of what a production designer's responsibilities and authority really should be has yet to be written. Whereas the credit Art Director is now relegated to the secondary roll call, it is presumed to be job akin to that of the camera operator or the key grip. There was a time when the art director was expected to do all those things that are now considered within the domain of the production designer. Perhaps the title Production Designer should be reconsidered and only be bestowed on someone who can: *"Enhance communication by visual means, produce settings that advance the story, use color for the enhancement of dramatic mood, be responsible for everything on the screen that doesn't move, and still find time to be a well-read and much-traveled gentleman who has broken bread in the poor man's hovel and wine glasses in the rich man's palace."*

The Filmmaking Team

To do what & with which & to whom

In an on-set interview, director Michael Winner, was asked if he thought of filmmaking as a team effort. "Yes, it is." he replied. Then, gesturing to the stage full of bustling technicians, added, "Of course, I think of a team effort as a lot of people doing as I tell them." This somewhat immodest answer is not altogether inaccurate. The motion-picture set is, as it must be, one of the last bastions of totalitarianism. When you consider that producing a motion picture is very much like starting a new business, it's amazing that it goes as smoothly as it does. The only real continuity from project to project is probably in the titles of the jobs. The following list isn't meant to define the work of the entire crew, but it will hopefully outline the relationship of each of them to the art director.

Writer

Although seldom seen by the art director, the writer has a profound influence on the visual concept of the picture. It is his descriptive stage direction and dialog that implant in the reader's imagination the environment, the mood, indeed, the color of the piece. When the writer is also the director, you have the bonus of the "horse's mouth" so to speak.

Producer

Historically, the producer was thought of as the money man. More recently, the title "producer" calls to mind the question, "Which one?" Ideally, the producer is that person who has mothered a project from story option through development and production right on through promotion and release. He must have the instincts necessary to judge the potential popularity of a project as well as the creative ability to select an appropriate director and cast. It is his word that is the last word in all production and creative decisions. This is a prerogative he seldom has to exercise if he has given his production manager and director the authority they deserve. Because of his deep involvement in the project, the producer can be counted on to provide some of the best research sources for any given project.

Director

Filmmaking is the director's art. Every person who reads the script has a mental image of the film, but it is the director's image that counts. The art director is expected to provide the director with a variety of visual styles from which he may select the setting for his work. The effective art director is one who can quickly embrace the director's concept and then create a "look" that projects that image.

Cast

Too many designers would define the cast as "those people who get in the way of the scenery." Avoid falling into the trap of exaggerating the value of the background. Remember, it's the actors who are reason for the medium's existence, and often a star will bring the reflection of his own personality to a role. This gives the art director another facet to explore in the creation of a visual concept.

Production Manager

As one might expect, the person responsible for budgeting and controlling the expenditure of a huge sum of money is going to be vitally concerned with the operation of the art department. Keep him fully informed of the status of current and anticipated construction expenses. Be prepared to give him changing budget figures as may be created by changes of schedule, inclement weather, changes of location, or script revisions. It is the production manager who approves the construction of each set on the show.

Production Coordinator

The person to whom everyone on the staff owes a debt of gratitude is this chief administrator of the production office. Telephone messages, correspondence, travel arrangements, hotel accommodations, call sheets, cast and crew lists, office supplies, telephones, time cards, charge accounts, deal memos, and the production-office coffee supply are but a few of the demands that cross her desk. She is often the one who holds the other end of the art director's leash: the beeper line.

Assistant Director

With the responsibility of keeping a shooting company running smoothly, the assistant director is vitally interested in the preparations being made by the art department. Keep him updated on the status of sets under construction, those being dressed, and especially cover sets. He is the one to give you the best estimate of when the company will be moving into a new set or location. Since he is also in charge of the call sheet, let him know what sets might need an extra greensman or a standby propmaker (carpenter).

Accountant

The construction coordinator and set decorator will usually have more contact with the accountant than the art director, whose needs for petty cash, charge accounts, and rentals are minimal compared to theirs. An efficient accountant can keep you in daily touch with your status relative to the construction budget. Sometimes it's necessary to have the accountant and the construction coordinator sit down and ferret out misplaced charges that may appear.

Casting Director

The casting director only rarely meets with the art director. The occasions that come to mind are when personal candid photos of actors are needed for set dressing, or when a cockpit or prop must be designed to conform to the size of the actor. Unless you have a niece who is an aspiring actress, you might do a whole show without seeing the casting director.

Publicist

It is only when the sets become a unique or significant aspect of the production that the publicist will look up the art director. If this does happen, it's a good idea to brief the producer on what you plan to say. Not everything that goes on behind the scenes is for public release. When it happens, enjoy your place in the sun. It's not often that off-camera personnel get a chance to blow their own horn.

Technical Advisor

The single greatest help in researching a show is the technical advisor. A good many shows require this kind of assistance. Try to get in as much pre-production time as possible with the advisor, because once shooting starts, you have lost him to the demands of the shooting company.

Transportation Coordinator

Aside from bearing the imposing task of shuttling this circus of a production company from place to place, the transportation coordinator also has the job of providing "picture" vehicles. The selection of these "props" is the concern of the art director as well as that of the property master. The painting, lettering, signing, and, in some cases, the modification of these vehicles are certainly the art department's responsibilities. Save your best painter to give the props and vehicles appropriate aging.

Stunt Coordinator

Most stunts require some degree of physical assistance. The special-effects team can usually meet these needs. And the property master will provide the incidental breakaway objects. When stunts become complicated, the stunt coordinator often needs continuity sketches (a storyboard) and special construction beyond the scope of the special-effects technicians—such as frames for safety nets, barriers ramps, and pits. Indeed, some sets are designed entirely around a particular stunt.

Special Effects

When the schedule calls for a full-time special-effects man, he can sometimes become an extra man for the art department to count on. If he is not involved in an effects sequence (fog, rain, explosions, stunts, etc.), he is usually nearby in the effects van and available to fix a sticking door or replace a traffic sign. His cooperation is essential when breakaway elements such as windows, handrails, or walls are built into the set. Scenes that call for "practical" units like fireplaces, showers, or sinks also become the concern of the special-effects team.

Location Manager

Aside from the duties described earlier, the location manager continues to function as liaison with location owners and local authorities. He is also an active part of the shooting company. He is usually the first person to arrive on location and often the only one with the key that the set-dressing crew needs to detail the set before the company arrives. If arrangements must be made for the security of a set on weekends or overnight, he can take care of that.

Script Supervisor

The constant presence of the script supervisor on the set makes this person one of the best sources of information about which portions of the set have been seen on camera.

The dailies, of course, are the best source, but time occasionally works against this method.

Film Editor

When shooting begins, the editor comes aboard to supervise the processing of exposed film, prepare dailies, and assemble filmed sequences. If a still photo from a scene is needed by the art director, the editor can provide an enlarged print made from a film clip. His real challenge, of course, comes in post-production.

I am reminded of a story related to me by prominent Hollywood producer Freddie Fields: While walking early one morning in London, Fields unexpectedly came upon his friend and fellow producer Dino DeLaurentis, whom he hadn't seen for some time. Fields was impressed with Dino's gushing enthusiasm. "Oh, Freddie, I've just finished the most beautiful film I've ever seen. It's wonderful, it's exciting, it brought tears to my eyes." When Freddie then knowingly asked him: "Can you save it in editing?" his immediate reply was, "Absolutely!"

Photo-Effects Coordinator

Shows or series that rely heavily on special photographic effects will have a photo-effects coordinator. This highly technical aspect of filmmaking requires a person familiar with the state of the art. A storyboard is almost a necessity if those concerned are to work toward the same result. Even though this consultant adopts the work that would normally be that of the art director, it is still the responsibility of the art director to maintain the visual concept of the show.

Director of Photography

It isn't by accident that the director of photography commands the respect he does on the stage. He is responsible for the images that appear on that strip of film. It is his creative use of cameras, film stock, lighting, lenses, filters, diffusers, camera angles, and moves that gives a mood and character to the story. The end results of all the art, technology, and talent that go into telling that story rest in his hands. It pays to have the director of photography involved in as many pre-production concept meetings as possible.

Gaffer

As part of the camera team, the gaffer's allegiance is to the director of photography. They have probably done many shows together and their communication is almost unspoken. The art director should try to have an early meeting with the gaffer. Some prefer lighting from scaffolding while others get better results from the floor. The brightness or illumination level will often effect decisions on colors, textures, and aging. Backings on stage differ in the space they require for front or back lighting.

Key Grip

The third member of the camera triumvirate is the key grip. Although it appears that the grip crew is another resource to call upon when a standby carpenter is needed, remember that the grips most often have their time occupied with laying dolly track, building platforms, or moving set walls. Building sets that are designed for easy manipulation goes a long way toward gaining the cooperation of the key grip when that occasional help is needed.

Sound Mixer

In the mind of a good sound mixer, a film is really an illustrated soundtrack. He wants that track to be perfect. The art director can make the sound man's life a lot easier in many ways. The selection of locations away from noise sources such as highways, fountains, or compressors is a good start. On stage, fluorescent light transformers should be made remote and platforms should be sound-deadened.

Property Master

Although not officially a part of the art department, the property master is one of the art director's most effective cohorts. His creative selection of hand props can bring a spark of reality to the set. See that he gets all the help he needs in aging those critical props.

They tell the story about the propman who forgot a piece of jewelry that was crucial to a scene. The director launched into a scathing reprimand. At the conclusion of this tirade, the propman turned and walked away. "Where do you think you're going?" asked the director. "To my prop box," replied the propman. "Do you have a piece there that'll work for us?" the director asked, hopefully. "No," said the propman, "my check book is there. I want to see if I have enough money to tell you to go to hell."

Wrangler

Westerns and period shows open new worlds of design for the art director. The property master often relies on the wrangler to supply wagons, gear, and tack. Inevitably, this results in the need for designs to modify or manufacture some of this equipment. Enjoy your venture into archeological reproduction.

Costume Designer

Costume designers are the kindred spirits of the art department. They are among the first to rap on the art director's door after coming on board. A good costume designer wants to make sure that his/her creations are mounted in the best possible setting. Often, medallions or logos must be designed before embroidered jackets or patches can be made. The need for this collaboration is obvious.

Costumer

Men's and women's costumers have a big enough chore keeping the actors in the proper wardrobe for each scene without having to worry about what clothing they have loaned out. So, even though this seems to be an excellent source for closet dressing and messy bedroom clutter, suggest that the set decorator find another source for this essential detailing.

Makeup Artist

Unless called upon to provide continuity sketches of a werewolf transformation, the art director probably won't meet the makeup artist until they find themselves reaching for the same tray at the caterer's truck. However, the advent of high-tech makeup appliances makes that storyboard situation more likely than ever.

Hair Stylist

Setting up the hair stylist with nice quarters on the corner of the stage may not be the most critical function of the art director, but it will pay off when you have to go directly from the stage to the awards ceremony and need that last-minute trim.

Standby Painter

Once the shooting company hits the stage, a function called "set operations" comes into play. A set painter is taken from the construction crew and assigned to the stage crew. There, he comes under the command of the director of photography. When not busy touching up wall seams, he can be counted on to age hand props or wardrobe. Some painters take to this task with enthusiasm; others would rather watch grass grow than spend a day with the production company. Make this choice carefully.

Standby Greensman

Not always a regular part of the production crew, the greensman is often an employee of the company providing the plant material. His tasks can vary from cutting limbs as shadow elements to draping grass mats over unwanted background objects. He is also part of set operations.

Craft Service

The duties of a craft-service person, when properly recognized, go beyond maintaining the coffee pot and snack table. He/she should really be that extra person that every craft occasionally needs. Setting up cast and crew chairs, vacuuming the set, or stopping pedestrian traffic would not be unusual requests to make of this jack-of-all-trades.

Post-Production Services

The art director's services pretty well wrap up with the end of principle photography. It is a rare situation that will require his post-production concern. Directing a second-camera unit to get establishing shots comes to mind. The more common occurrence would be the coordination of filming miniatures, special optical effects, or, in rare instances, designing titles and credits.

So, with this never-identical assemblage of filmmaking talent, somehow each project is completed, and in much the same way that a new business venture is launched, the film is released. The degree of success it achieves will, in one way or another, effect the lives of everyone listed in the credits. It may be a mercurial system upon which to base a career, but one has to approach it with eternal optimism. As an example of this optimism, let me relate my awakening to the genuine enthusiasm and dedication that work in this magical world can engender.

I hadn't seen my good friend and talented artist John Jensen in some time, so it was with pleasure that I went to the Disney Studios to meet him for lunch. He was working as the illustrator and continuity artist for the live-action feature *Condorman,* which involved a young man's attempt to fly like a bird. The walls of John's office were literally covered with drawings of our hero wearing various wing-like attachments and contrivances enabling him to soar unfettered alongside his avian inspirations. The drawings required a great deal of ingenuity on John's part as he had to design the various sprockets, leverage devices, and pulleys employed in this young man's invention. When I expressed my admiration for his creative efforts, this enthusiastic artist confided in me: "Ward, I think he'll really be able to fly."

The First Time Out

"You can't send the kid up in a crate like that."

We have all experienced the "first times" in many endeavors, whether it's riding a bike or taking over as the CEO of a Fortune 500 company. Doing your first show as an art director falls somewhere between these two possibilities in importance—but way beyond this scale in anxiety. Let's take a moment to explore that hypothetical first solo outing. You probably *won't* have the support of a film-studio environment (mill, scene dock, sign shop, prop house, etc.)—*nor* an assistant art director, *nor* a set designer, *nor* a full-time construction crew, *nor* an adequate budget. What you *will* be bringing to this project is a solid background in art—*and* a moderate knowledge of film production, *and* a boundless enthusiasm.

Assuming that you are fairly conversant with the information covered in this book, now start adapting these principles to match the scope of your project. No research budget? Use the public library, the historical society, check with friends who are familiar with the subject of your story. No money for expensive locations or location brokers? Check with the owners of vacant buildings of the type you need. Some will welcome the windfall of a moderate location fee. In areas where filming is a novelty, owners can be induced to cooperate just by assuring them that you are adequately insured (a must), and they can sometimes be given work as extras in the show. When there is no official location manager, the production manager fills the gap by preparing contracts and obtaining permits.

Almost every location will require some touch-up or modification (if not before filming, certainly thereafter), so try to carry on the show at least a carpentry foreman and a film-wise painter. When the time comes to build a set piece, such as a wild wall to screen off an unwanted view into an adjoining room or a foreground window unit, then your foreman can assemble the necessary men and materials. And, if your show presents the opportunity to build an occasional interior set or a location exterior, you can then get serious about some design and construction time.

Stage space will probably not be a professional soundstage, but by following the criteria noted in the discussion of distant locations, you should be able to find a suitable location. Sometime that "stage" turns up in unlikely places. I remember the time when we rented a vacant floor in a downtown Los Angeles office building because there were some offices we could use in our story. In the large empty space adjacent to the offices, I built two other sets that were supposedly miles away. This eliminated a move by the production company and saved on the cost of renting another location. Once a location has been selected, always survey the area around it for potential additional sets.

Sketch, sketch, sketch. There is no better way to get your ideas across than through a drawing. Sketches keep the director informed of the layout of the sets and locations so that he can better prepare for staging the action. (On most productions, directors expect and deserve neatly scaled drawings or "director's plans" of each location on script-size pages.) Sketches show the location manager what you mean when you want him to find a place with Tudor arches and linen-fold paneling. Sketches give the decorator an idea of what kind of canopies you have in mind for that Mexican market-place. Sketches show the stunt man what part of that billboard is balsa wood and what part is sheet metal. He will thank you for it!

With the current abundance of builder's home centers, it is becoming more convenient to build sets away from studio facilities. With drawings made by a local draftsman, the construction foreman can make a material takeoff and give you a pretty good idea of the set cost before ever committing to start work. The conventional materials like lumber, drywall and plywood are going to hold pretty constant in cost, but things like ceramic tile, wallpapers, floor coverings, cabinet work, and hardware can vary five-fold. You would also be well advised to check out some of the wallpapers available with photographic finishes of stone and brick etc. However, when the texture of the surface becomes critical, the added cost of studio-made fiberglass brick "skins" may be worth it. (Most Hollywood studios now sell these to the public.)

Painting and aging are really what art direction is all about. On most locations, you will be able to find journeymen painters, but rare indeed are the painters trained to paint and age motion-picture sets. Occasionally, a local man, seeing the challenge, will be able to experiment and do a passable job. The mistakes on the road to perfection, however, can be horrendous. Once they learn to make alligator-crazed surfaces, multiple-coat build-ups (roping), wood graining, multicolored water stains, flaking exterior paint (graduated up from the splash line), block-aging around door jambs, naturally weathered raw wood, and a nicotine glaze, then they can start to call themselves "studio painters."

Signs will drive you crazy. Don't be discouraged and think that your problems with signs are unique. We have all gone through it. Signs will always look too fresh. There will never be a convenient way to hang them, and signs that really should be painted directly on doors, windows, and the sides of vehicles will somehow always end up being done on plaques, decals, or magnetic skins. The most you can hope for is to find a local sign shop that still has a man capable of lettering without a computer. Always allow enough time after receiving the sign to get it properly aged. And if you can come up with an acceptable alternative to the typical movie-sign phone prefix of "555," you might win a medal.

As you get into the construction phase, it will be worth your while to stand guard over your fragile budget. Usually there are separate accounts set up for construction vehicles, set operations (standby painter and greensman), patching and striking locations, manufacturing of props and set dressing, and grip work (tarp frames and scaffolding). Location accountants can't be expected to recognize the difference between plywood for set walls or for dolly flooring when the bill comes in unless someone tells them. I've already mentioned the prop-truck shelves and that access road to the *Rio Conchos* site, so be alert if you want to still have funds for that crucial final set. By the way, one source of money sometimes available for set construction is that location fee that was saved when it was decided to build the set instead of renting a location.

In the discussion of backings, I covered the conventional ways of backing up windows. There are alternatives. How often have I struggled over the placement of a backing only to find in dailies that the window is just a hot glow on the screen. With the cooperation of the cameraman and when the view out the window is not critical to the story, it is possible to "burn out" the window by placing a sheet of translucent vellum on the outside frame. A sheer or lace interior curtain helps complete this effect. Slatted blinds will often serve the same purpose. In a pinch, you might even check the available photo-mural wallpapers, but now you will probably be involved with a cost that makes a conventional rental backing reasonable.

The backing challenge for night sequences offers a little more flexibility. All the camera will see out the windows is what we want it to see. A black backing allows the use of peanut lights on grip stands, a cut-out profile of the horizon (mounted at eye level, of course), or foreground greens. If an evening sky glow is desired, you might want to substitute a night-gray backing, in which case the horizon profile becomes mandatory. When tarping-in a real location to shoot day-for-night, it helps the effect to include some greens in the enclosed area. Don't forget additional off-camera space for the gaffer's lamps.

Of course, there'll be no budget for post-production special effects. Consider some of the in-the-camera effects that have been used over the years: "Under-cranking" and "over-cranking" are the terms that have been used to describe accelerated motion and slow motion effects. When photographing miniatures, slow-motion should be used to give inertia and a realistic sense of gravity to the image. Characters can be "popped" in and out of the picture by having everyone freeze as the actor takes or leaves his position. The editor simply snips out the frames that reveal the actor moving into place.

The term "poor man's process" refers to a moving vehicle shot without the help of a rear-projection screen. To be effective, it generally requires two conditions: that it be a night sequence and that the vehicle be relatively enclosed so that the camera only catches glimpses of the passing terrain. With a solid black "duvateen" backing, lights and shadows can be manipulated to give the illusion of motion. It's a poor substitute for the effects possible today, but even now, it is sometimes used on minimum-budget features and movies made for television.

Dressing a minimum-budget project requires all the inventiveness your decorator can muster. The optimistic hope is that all the locations you find will be appropriately dressed. The only safety net you have is the willingness of local merchants to rent furniture and accessories to the film company. On locations outside the reach of prop houses, you will come to thank the world of flea markets and thrift stores. When purchasing new props and dressing from established dealers, the potential for exposure of their product on the screen or television often induces them to make very generous, if not gratis deals. Also, with the cooperation of your producer, you can sometimes offer them screen credit. However, this is a bargaining chip not to be used loosely. The ramifications are significant.

Another hint for your decorator is that he or she should attend dailies—especially when they include work of a heavily dressed set or location. Things such as lamps or pictures that didn't get filmed are still available to dress future sets. When money is spent to buy or rent dressing that never appears on camera, it is a shame. Lamps are an especially valuable set dressing element. Most directors of photography like to compose with visible light sources, so you can't have too many lamps in reserve. The same holds true for foreground elements. Camera moves are particularly interesting when the perspective is accentuated by foreground movement.

Finally, it's time for the wrap party, and you can proudly say that you put all the money that was entrusted to you up there on the screen where it counted. Who knows? This might be the project that opens the door to that big high-budget feature that we all dream of. And of course you'll rate the credit Production Designer. Here's wishing yo the best of luck in your new career.

The
Ten Commandments
Of
Art Direction

All the camera sees is the last coat of paint.

Don't cheat (unless you have to).

Signs of protest are best done by amateurs.

The horizon is always at eye level.

It don't mean a thing if it ain't got that look.

Dirty old hand props need aging too.

Be there when it's still just lines on the floor.

If it feels good, do it.

The presentation is a bit of show business.

Show no set before it's time.

Ten Commandments of Art Direction

All the camera sees is the last coat of paint.

When it looks like the world has gone crazy and you find an artillery piece being shaped out of wood or log walls being cast in fiberglass, put your faith in those wonderful technicians on the paint crew. The eye of the camera really doesn't care if that cornice molding is made of styrofoam, wood, or limestone.

Don't cheat (unless you have to).

Having just extolled the "last coat of paint" theory, let me be quick to sing the virtues of the real thing. Whenever possible, use the genuine article. It is usually easier, cheaper, and more adaptable to the inevitable last-minute changes in front of the camera. "Let's crash the runaway wagon into that log cabin."

Signs of protest are best done by amateurs.

Even the most picture-wise of the experienced studio craftsmen have a problem with creating amateurish work. If you want that farm shed to have just the right character, you don't give the job to your best propmaker and tell him to just slap it up. Give it to the trainee and tell him to do his very best.

The horizon is always at eye level.

Have faith in the maxim that, as earthlings, we are sentenced to forever having the line of the horizon follow us up, even as we ascend our tallest buildings. It's tough enough making some of the tired old rental backings believable without taking on a battle with the laws of nature to boot.

It don't mean a thing if it ain't got that look.

Every decision we make as designers should be based on the overall concept we have established for the show. The quest for style doesn't stop with the selection of the show's color palette and the decision to never see satin except in the bordello sequence. Be consistent. If you've started in C major, don't switch to D minor.

Dirty old hand props need aging, too.

Aging might justifiably be defined as the "art" in art direction. This is the finishing touch that will lift a set out of the ordinary into sacred realm of the believable. Don't let the spell be broken by a car that looks like it got too close to a painter cleaning his brushes or by a toolbox that has never known the indignity of a mislaid wipe rag. Everything needs aging.

Be there when it's still just lines on the floor.

You will never find enough time to do all that you have to do. Too often, when you get around to looking at work in progress, the river has risen and you're still shopping for sandbags. Whether it's a new set being laid out on a stage or crew arriving for the first time at a location to be revamped, meet them there and be sure they're cutting the skylight into the right room.

If it feels good, do it.

Learn to trust your instincts. Not all of our decisions can be the results of calculated logic. That first reaction, no matter how far-fetched, is still an intellectual reflex based on your serendipitous experiences and might very well offer a better answer to a situation than a 15 page report from a blue-ribbon government committee.

The presentation is a bit of show business.

Don't ever assume that, because you're all looking at the same script, you are therefore all visualizing the same film. Even after screening similar films and discussing pictorial research, it is not until you are all looking at the same models, illustrations, and storyboards that the real visual impact starts to gel. Give these visual-concept meetings the moment they deserve.

Show no set before its time.

A trick known to most art directors who have had the good fortune to work with really creative painters is to subtly introduce other colors into a set by revealing undercoats of previous colors when aging. A room may be tan with white trim now, but crazing on the doors will reveal a hint of turquoise, and a water-stained wall can have traces of yellow or even magenta. The last thing you want a director to see is this set in its turquoise, yellow, or magenta mode.

Suggested Reading

Hollywood Art, Art Direction in the Days of the Great Studios. Beverly Heisner (Jefferson, NC: McFarland & Co., 1990).

Designing Dreams. Donald Albrecht (New York: Harper & Row, 1986).

Film Design. Terence Marner (London: Tantivy Press, 1974).

Caligari's Cabinet and Other Grand Illusions. Leon Barsacq (Boston: New York Graphic Society, 1976).

The Haunted Screen. Lotte Eisner (Berkley: University of California Press, 1969).

What a Producer Does: The Art of Moviemaking (Not the Business). Buck Houghton (Los Angeles: Silman-James Press, 1991).

My Work in Films. Eugene Lourie (San Diego: Harcourt Brace, 1985).

The Art of Hollywood Thames Television Exhibit. (London: MacDermott & Chant Ltd., 1979).

Designed for Film, The Hollywood Art Director. Mary Corless, *Film Comment,* May/June 1978, *p.27.*

The Film Director's Team. Alain Silver & Elizabeth Ward (Los Angeles: Silman-James Press, 1992).

Film Directing Shot by Shot. Steven D. Katz (Studio City: Michael Wiese Productions, 1991).

Acknowledgments

A year ago, I never would have believed that I would someday be pondering how best to acknowledge the help I had received in writing a book on art direction. Now that the time has arrived, I only wish that I had taken better notes in chronicling the efforts of the many friends and associates who encouraged and assisted me on my maiden voyage.

Since I've already mentioned my wife and son in the introduction, I would be most ungrateful if I didn't point out the inspiration so generously given by my daughters Valerie and Pamela. Nearly a part of the family now that she has spent so much time reading and critiquing these pages is my good friend and talented fellow art director Peg McClellan. Other designers whose help was welcomed but didn't get singled out in the text: Tracy Bousman, Bill Ross, Dennis Washington, Bill Malley, Jan Scott, Mark Mansbridge, Frank Grieco and Bernie Cutler.

In addition to those already cited in the book's text, I want to note here the help of the following organizations and individuals. Susan Agnoff for her research assistance and unflagging encouragement; Terry Ward, Pacific Studios; Linda

Maher and Carol Cullen, Margaret Herrick Library of the Academy of Motion Picture Arts and Sciences; Lynn Coakly, J.C. Backings, Larry McCallister at Paramount Pictures; Ross Sluyter, Photo Backgrounds; Buck Houghton, producer; Bob Pincus, Warner Bros. Studios; Robert Radnitz, producer; William DeCinces and Jamie Fleming, Universal Studios, Al DiNoble and John Swallow, Pacific Data Images; Carol Walton, Foresight Resources Corp.

The real heroes in bringing this project to fruition are the guiding lights of the Silman-James Press: Gwen Feldman and Jim Fox. Thank you both for helping this neophyte writer along the unmarked trail to the printer's press.

Index